PSYCHOLOGY LIBRARY EDITIONS:
PSYCHOLOGY OF READING

Volume 4

THE PSYCHOLOGY OF READING AND SPELLING DISABILITIES

THE PSYCHOLOGY OF READING AND SPELLING DISABILITIES

A.F. JORM

Routledge
Taylor & Francis Group
LONDON AND NEW YORK

First published in 1983 by Routledge & Kegan Paul plc

This edition first published in 2018
by Routledge
2 Park Square, Milton Park, Abingdon, Oxon OX14 4RN

and by Routledge
711 Third Avenue, New York, NY 10017

Routledge is an imprint of the Taylor & Francis Group, an informa business

British Library Cataloguing in Publication Data
A catalogue record for this book is available from the British Library

ISBN: 978-1-138-08065-2 (Set)
ISBN: 978-0-203-70345-8 (Set) (ebk)
ISBN: 978-1-138-08842-9 (Volume 4) (hbk)
ISBN: 978-1-315-10985-5 (Volume 4) (ebk)

Publisher's Note
The publisher has gone to great lengths to ensure the quality of this reprint but points out that some imperfections in the original copies may be apparent.

Disclaimer
The publisher has made every effort to trace copyright holders and would welcome correspondence from those they have been unable to trace.

The psychology of reading and spelling disabilities

A.F. Jorm

Routledge & Kegan Paul

London, Boston, Melbourne and Henley

First published in 1983
by Routledge & Kegan Paul plc
39 Store Street, London WC1E 7DD,
9 Park Street, Boston, Mass. 02108, USA,
296 Beaconsfield Parade, Middle Park,
Melbourne 3206, Australia, and
Broadway House, Newtown Road,
Henley-on-Thames, Oxon RG9 1EN
Set in Times Roman and Bold
and printed in Great Britain by
Unwin Brothers Limited, The Gresham Press,
Old Woking, Surrey GU22 9LH

Library of Congress Cataloging in Publication Data

Jorm, A. F., 1951–

The psychology of reading and spelling disabilities.
(International library of psychology)
Bibliography: p.
Includes index.
1. Reading disability. 2. Spelling disability.
3. Reading, Psychology of. I. Title. II. Series.
L1050.5.J62 1982 428.4'2 82-20463

ISBN 0-7100-9344-6

Contents

Preface and acknowledgments

This preface, although appearing at the beginning of the book, was in fact the last section to be written. From this vantage point, it is hard not to reflect back on how it all began. So I will end by giving an account of this book's beginnings.

The historical origins of this book lie initially in a PhD thesis entitled *Components of Reading Disability* submitted at the University of New South Wales in 1972. The author of this thesis, Ian Firth, had laboured for many years on the work (seven years, I think), and he lost interest in it after it was completed. Although the thesis has never been published, it has exerted some influence on reading researchers.

During his PhD candidature, Firth had a succession of supervisors, the final one being Don McNicol who, in 1975, became my own PhD supervisor. It was Don McNicol who introduced me to Firth's thesis. Firth's ideas had a considerable influence on me and became the basis for much of my subsequent thinking on reading disability. This influence is apparent in a number of the chapters of this book.

During the two years I was a PhD student I worked out my own views on reading disabilities which went considerably beyond Firth's ideas. In 1977, after taking up a position at Deakin University, I gave a talk on the subject to a group of special education teachers. John McNeil, who was a visitor to Deakin from the University of California at Riverside, asked to come along and hear the talk. He afterwards told me that I ought to write up the contents of the talk for publication. John McNeil has a rather sanguine temperament, and is prone to optimistic appraisals, but I took his suggestion seriously. The paper appeared as an article in the journal *Cognition.* This article evoked considerable interest, both positive and negative. I was besieged with reprint requests and received quite a few letters commenting favourably on it. Two commentaries on the article have subsequently been published, one in *Cognition* and one in the *Australian Journal of Psychology.* These were basically critical (not without some justification) and aimed to present alternative points of view. I afterwards heard that quite a number of commentaries on the article were submitted to *Cognition,* although not published.

After the publication of the *Cognition* article, I thought I would like to write a much expanded version. With this aim in mind, I applied for a semester's study leave in the latter half of 1980. This leave was spent at the Center for the Study of Reading of the University of Illinois. The Center kindly provided me with an office, which I shared with a number of other visitors who passed through that semester. I found the company of those people quite stimulating and learned something from each of them. By the time my stay at Illinois was over I had managed to complete a first draft. I cannot say I enjoyed writing it. My relationship with the manuscript was something of a love-hate one. Writing does not come easily to me, so every word had to be wrenched out with some effort. However, whenever a chapter was finished I did gain some satisfaction through the relief that it was over. The Center for the Study of Reading, with its emphasis on the study of comprehension, made its own impact on the book. The chapter on Reading Comprehension Disabilities is much bigger than it would have been had I written it in Australia.

A major characteristic of this book is that each chapter argues a particular point of view. If a reviewer were to criticize the book, he or she would undoubtedly make the accusation that it is oversimplified in its account. In many ways it is, but this simplification reflects my own bias as to how evidence is best integrated. It has been said that there are two kinds of people in the world, the simplifiers and the complexifiers. I am undoubtedly a simplifier. The challenge to me in looking at a confusing and complex research area like reading and spelling disabilities is to search out the thread of consistency which lies behind it all. Never mind that the evidence is a little too fuzzy to support fully the apparent consistencies. I believe that in the long run these consistencies will provide the basis for extending our account of the problem to cover the currently discrepant evidence.

A second characteristic of the book is that it looks at the topic from a researcher's rather than a practitioner's point of view. Essentially, it is designed to convey current research work on reading and spelling disabilities to the non-researcher. This includes the practitioner, the student, and the parent. Although many books already exist on the topic of reading disabilities, these are generally written from the practitioner's point of view, and, unfortunately, reflect little of the understanding researchers have gained in recent years of the reading process or reading disabilities. I felt that a gap existed which needed to be filled. Although it is not a how-to-do-it book on the diagnosis or treatment of literacy problems, it nevertheless has considerable relevance to those who are interested in such immediately practical issues. I have no doubt that the practical benefits of the current wave of reading research will be felt before the end of the century.

A book such as this could not be written without the help and co-operation of many people. Firstly, there is Deakin University which provided me with leave for the purpose. Professor Iain Wallace was particularly helpful in this regard. Then there is the Center for the Study of Reading, particularly through its administrator Betty Yankwich, which provided me with facilities during my period of leave. Upon return to Deakin several people read the draft manuscript and provided helpful comments and suggestions: David Share, Rod Maclean and Russell Matthews. Sonia Lappin was responsible for expertly typing two versions of the manuscript. Lastly, there was the encouragement of my two good friends Betty and Ruth, who are my wife and daughter respectively. Although this book would probably have been written six months quicker without them, life would not have been as enjoyable in the process.

The author and publishers would like to thank the following for permission to reprint copyright material: Daniel Hier, Marjorie LeMay, Peter B. Rosenberger and Vincent P. Perlo, 'Developmental dyslexia', *Archives of Neurology*, 1978, vol. 35, February, fig. 1, p. 91, copyright 1978, American Medical Association; C. Spring and C. Capps, 'Encoding speed, rehearsal, and probed recall of dyslexic boys', *Journal of Educational Psychology*, 1974, vol. 66, no. 5, p. 782, fig. 1, copyright 1974 by the American Psychological Association, reprinted/adapted by permission of the author; D. Shankweiler, I.Y. Liberman, L.S. Mark, C.A. Fowler and F.W. Fischer, 'The speech code and learning to read', *Journal of Experimental Psychology: Human Learning and Memory*, 1979, vol. 5, no. 6, November, p. 535, fig. 1, copyright 1979 by the American Psychological Association, reprinted/adapted by permission of the author; Anthony Jorm, 'Effect of Word Imagery on Reading Performance as a function of reader ability', *Journal of Educational Psychology*, 1977, vol. 69, no. 1, p. 51, copyright 1977 by the American Psychological Association; P. Rozin *et al.*, 'American Children with reading problems can easily learn to read English represented by Chinese characters', *Science*, 1971, vol. 171, pp. 1264–7, fig. 2, March, copyright 1971 by the American Association for the Advancement of Science; Frank Vellutino, Joseph A. Steger, C.J. Harding and Formen Phillips, 'Verbal vs. non-verbal paired associates learning in poor and normal readers', *Neuropsychologia*, 1975, vol. 13, p. 77, fig. 1 and M. Rutter and W. Yule, 'The concept of specific reading retardation', *Journal of Child Psychology and Psychiatry*, 1975, vol. 16, p. 185, fig. 1, copyright 1975, Pergamon Press Ltd; Geoff S. Einon (ed.), 'An EEG record', *Introduction to the Nervous System*, Open University Press, 1974, p. 17, copyright © 1974, The Open University Press; K. Conners, 'Cortical visual evoked response in children with learning disorders', *Psychophysiology*, 1970, vol. 7, p. 421, fig. 2; J.W. Pichert and R.C. Anderson, 'Taking different perspectives on a story', *Journal of Educational Psychology*, 1977, vol. 69, pp. 309-15; A. White Franklin and S. Naidoo (eds), *Assessment and Teaching of Dyslexic Children*, The Invalid Children's Aid Association, £1.75; J.E. Sweeney and B.P. Rourke, 'Neuropsychological significance of phonetically accurate and phonetically inaccurate spelling errors in younger and older retarded readers, *Brain and Language*, 1978, vol. 6, p. 218, fig. 1; F.R. Vellutino, R.M. Pruzek, J.A. Steger and V. Meshoulam, 'Immediate visual recall in poor and normal readers as a function of orthographic linguistic familiarity', *Cortex*, 1973, vol. 9, p. 373, fig. 1.

1 Varieties of reading and spelling disability

The problem of reading and spelling disabilities

Failure to achieve an adequate standard of literacy is generally recognised as being a major social problem in western societies. In a technologically advanced society, in which written language is all pervasive, a certain degree of reading and writing skills is absolutely necessary for survival. A person who is lacking in literacy skills is severely hampered in the range of educational and occupational choices he or she can make in life. Even today's leisure activities often demand a reasonable level of reading and writing skills.

Problems with literacy have secondary consequences as well. With such a high value placed on literacy skills in our society, the child who fails to achieve as expected may become frustrated with formal education, may develop feelings of personal inadequacy, and may even react by engaging in anti-social behaviour at school. There are also secondary effects on the parents and teachers. They will inevitably feel disappointed that the child has failed to achieve; they may also feel helpless and inadequate because they cannot find a solution; and they may even feel guilty because they believe themselves to be at fault for the child's difficulties. In the long run, these secondary effects may become almost as great a problem as the initial literacy difficulties which produced them.

Despite the importance of literacy difficulties, we still have very little understanding of the causes and cures of such problems. Anyone who looks for professional guidance on what to do about severe and persistent literacy problems is likely to be given conflicting diagnoses, labels and prescriptions. However, this unfortunate situation may be rapidly changing. Perhaps the major reason for the slow progress to date is that there was very little fundamental understanding of the processes involved in *normal* reading and spelling. It almost goes without saying that we will never understand reading and spelling disabilities until we have worked out some of the details of what is going on in normal reading and spelling. However, up until a decade ago researchers studying literacy problems were trying to do exactly that. Apart from some pioneering efforts early in the century, research into the normal reading process really only got underway in the 1970s, and research into the normal spelling process has been even later in coming. However, the research which has been carried out on normal reading and spelling so far is already making significant contributions to our understanding of disabilities.

Not only has our understanding of reading and spelling processes increased, but our understanding of cognitive processes in general has increased as well. As we will see, disabilities can result from deficits in the basic cognitive processes which underlie the complex skills of reading and spelling. Therefore, a fundamental knowledge of these basic cognitive processes is a prerequisite for an understanding of reading and spelling disabilities. Again, some real advances may be occurring on this front.

Perhaps the major difference between this book and previous treatments of the same topic is that it seeks an understanding of reading and spelling disabilities in terms of these recent advances in cognitive psychology.

Some basic distinctions

Before launching into a more detailed exposition of reading and spelling disabilities we need to make some basic distinctions and agree upon some terminology. It hardly needs to be pointed out that reading and spelling are very complex processes and that disabilities in these processes can arise in a number of different ways. One initial distinction which can be made is between loss of literacy skills after they have been acquired through some sort of damage to the brain, and failure to acquire adequate literacy skills during the course of otherwise normal development. The loss of literacy skills through brain damage is generally known as *acquired dyslexia* and is generally seen in adults rather than children. In fact, there are many different varieties of acquired dyslexia. They result from damage to different regions of the brain and involve deficiencies in different components of the reading or spelling process. There has been quite a lot of research into acquired dyslexia in recent years, but this type of disability is not dealt with in this book. The reader interested in finding out more about acquired dyslexia should consult Marshall and Newcombe (1973) or Coltheart, Patterson and Marshall (1980).

The other broad category of reading and spelling disabilities, which involves failure to acquire these skills initially, is the topic of this book. These are generally known as *developmental* disabilities. Several types of developmental disabilities can be distinguished. First, there is a distinction between the child who is poor at reading but also generally backward intellectually, and the child who is poorer at reading than would be expected from his or her general intellectual performance.

Rutter and Yule (1975) have used the term *general reading backwardness* to refer to the child whose reading disability occurs in the context of overall poor performance and the term *specific reading retardation* to describe the child with a disability specifically in reading. As an example, a child who is mentally retarded and poor at reading would fall into the category of general reading backwardness, while a child who is intellectually bright but has not achieved as expected in reading would fall into the category of specific reading retardation. The concept of specific reading retardation is somewhat similar to the popular concept of *developmental dyslexia*. However, it has a number of advantages over the traditional dyslexia concept. Undoubtedly the major advantage is that it is not so loosely and vaguely defined. Rutter and Yule (1975) have proposed a quite stringent method for defining specific reading retardation using a child's scores on reading achievement and intelligence tests. The other advantage of the concept of specific retardation is that it does not carry any connotations that the deficit necessarily has a purely biological basis, as the concept of dyslexia seems to.

A further distinction which can be drawn is between those children who are good at reading single words but fail to comprehend text adequately, and those who are poor at both reading single words and comprehending text. This distinction has been made by Cromer (1970) who uses the term *difference poor reader* to refer to the children deficient in comprehension but not in single word reading. This terminology reflects the fact that these children exhibit a difference between their performance at reading comprehension and their performance at reading single words. Cromer refers to the children with problems on both single words and comprehension as *deficit poor readers*, but this concept appears to be basically similar to Rutter and Yule's (1975) specific reading retardation. In this book, we will use the simple term *comprehension disability* to refer to readers whose deficit is specific to reading comprehension.

These various types of developmental reading disability are summarised in Table 1.1. As can be seen from this table, the different types of reading disability vary according to how general or specific the problem is. General reading backwardness involves problems in both reading comprehension and reading single words as well as low overall intelligence. Specific reading retardation involves problems with both aspects of reading, but normal ability in other respects. Lastly, comprehension disability involves problems specifically in the area of reading comprehension, with adequate reading of single words and adequate intelligence.

So far we have only dealt with different types of reading disability. However, we can also distinguish between types of developmental spelling disability. As might be expected, children with spelling difficulties generally have problems with reading as well. However, there is a small minority of children whose spelling performance is far worse than one would expect from someone of their reading ability. The children whose spelling difficulties are also accompanied by a reading disability will be referred to as *reading-and-spelling retardates,* while the children with difficulties specifically in spelling will be referred to as *spelling-only retardates.* The characteristics of these two types of spelling disability are summarised in Table 1.2. These two varieties of spelling disability obviously overlap with the varieties of reading disability summarised in Table 1.1. For example, children who are specific reading retardates will generally also be reading-and-spelling retardates. The differing terminology is used

Table 1.1 Varieties of disability in reading

	Deficiencies present		
Type of disability	Intelligence	Reading of single words	Comprehension of text
General reading backwardness	Yes	Yes	Yes
Specific reading retardation	No	Yes	Yes
Comprehension disabilities	No	No	Yes

depending on whether the primary focus of concern is the reading disability or the spelling disability. Hereafter, the terminology most appropriate for the topic of discussion (reading or spelling) will be used, without any implication that two entirely different disabilities are being discussed.

In the remaining chapters of this book, each of these types of reading or spelling disability is examined in detail. We will attempt to clarify which components of the normal reading or spelling process are deficient in these types of disabilities and will look at the possible reasons for these deficiencies.

We begin by looking in detail at the problem of specific reading retardation. Specific reading retardation has excited a lot of interest among researchers because of the seeming paradox of a child who has difficulty with reading and yet is intelligent in other respects. Unfortunately, general reading backwardness has generated far less interest, even though it is just as serious a problem. Because much less is known about general reading backwardness, the next few chapters concentrate mainly on specific reading retardation.

Table 1.2 Varieties of disability in spelling

	Deficiencies present	
Type of disability	Reading of single words	Spelling
Reading-and-spelling retardation	Yes	Yes
Spelling-only retardation	No	Yes

2 Specific reading retardation: The social context

In this chapter we will look at some of the basic social characteristics of children with specific reading retardation. We will see that specific reading retardation is not equally distributed throughout the population. It occurs more frequently in certain types of communities, in certain types of families, and in certain types of schools. Furthermore, it is not equally common amongst males and females. We will also see that children with specific reading retardation frequently have other sorts of major problems as well; social behavior problems as well as academic problems in subjects other than reading. Finally, we will look at the long term prospects for the retarded reader.

The importance of epidemiological studies

Despite the seeming importance of knowing about the social context of specific reading retardation, very little reliable information was available on this topic two decades ago. The reason is that most studies of reading problems are carried out on children who are referred to a clinic for special assessment or remediation. Researchers quite commonly compare these clinic children to other children of the same age who have not been referred for reading problems. Although research of this type has yielded many valuable findings, it suffers from the problem that the children who are referred to clinics may not be typical of children with reading problems in the general population. For example, if it were found (as it commonly is) that many more boys are referred to clinics for reading problems than are girls, we might conclude that boys have reading problems more often than girls. However, it could just be that parents or teachers show more concern over reading problems in boys than in girls, so more boys are referred to clinics. As another example, it is often reported that children who are referred to clinics for reading problems tend to have emotional disturbances as well. Again, it might be that children who have *both* a reading problem and an emotional disturbance are more likely to be referred to a clinic than children who have *only* a reading problem. In other words, the social characteristics of clinic samples may reflect the biases of the people who refer children to these clinics, rather than real differences between retarded and normal readers. The only way to get a true indication of the social characteristics of retarded readers is to study a total population of children and select out everybody who is a retarded reader. Studies of this general type are sometimes carried out by medical researchers interested in the social circumstances of people who have some disease or other, and are referred to as *epidemiological studies*. These studies are expensive and time-consuming to carry out so they are done all too infrequently.

Fortunately, a series of major epidemiological studies has been carried out on populations of English children in recent years, although similar studies have yet to be done in other countries. The English studies looked at reading retardation as well as a number of other childhood problems and have provided by far the clearest picture of the social circumstances associated with specific reading retardation. Most of the findings discussed in this chapter come from this series of epidemiological studies.

The incidence of specific reading retardation

A very basic question that is often asked is : How frequent is reading retardation? It is certainly not very hard to find answers to this question in the professional literature. Even newspapers frequently contain reports that some leading authority or other says there is an X per cent incidence of the problem. Unfortunately, the Xs typically vary widely from one leading authority to another. It is not very hard to find estimates varying from a low of 1 per cent to a high of 20 per cent. Incidence figures such as these are often used to show that reading problems are much more frequent in some countries (typically Britain and USA) than in others (such as Finland, Germany, or Japan). Although claims such as these may sound quite plausible, they are seldom based on any hard evidence. At worst, they may be simply guestimates that somebody dreamed up. At best, they may be based on some research evidence, but the criteria used for what constitutes a reading problem are not precisely specified. The basic problem with specifying the incidence of reading retardation lies in how the problem is defined. We must remember that retarded readers do not differ in any qualitative way from normal readers in terms of scores on a reading achievement test; they simply achieve at a quantitatively lower level. So in defining reading retardation we are simply selecting an arbitrary cutoff point and saying that we will regard anyone below that point as a retarded reader. It is basically for this reason that statements to the effect that X per cent of the school population have reading problems are of doubtful worth. In point of fact, even with the best research evidence it is possible to produce any incidence of reading problems we wish simply by altering our criterion in the appropriate way. For example, if we define any child who is below average is being a retarded reader, we might have an incidence as high as 50 per cent. On the other hand, by setting a suitably low cutoff point, we could create an incidence of less than 1 per cent.

The same problem arises when comparisons are made across countries. We have no way of knowing whether the criteria used to define reading retardation are the same in different countries. Considering the wide variation in estimates of incidence which are found within a single country, it seems highly likely that there would be as much variation across countries. Thus, Makita's (1968) claim that reading problems are extremely rare amongst children in Japan may reflect a true state of affairs or it may simply reflect a reluctance on the part of Japanese teachers to label children in this way; we have no way of knowing.

Clearly what is needed is some objective and clearly defined criterion for classifying children as being retarded readers. Although any such criterion will of necessity be arbitrary, it will still allow us to make statements about the incidence of reading retardation within and between communities. Rutter and Yule (1975) have advocated the use of a statistical procedure called multiple regression for this purpose. The exact details of this procedure need not concern us here, but basically multiple regression allows us to use information about a child's age and intelligence to make a prediction about what we would expect his or her reading level to be. In fact, multiple regression will allow us to make optimal predictions, so that we will tend to have the smallest errors possible in making them. Of course, in very many instances a child will be reading at roughly the level we would expect, but sometimes a child will be reading either much better or much worse than we would expect. Only when children are reading very much worse than expected are they regarded as retarded readers. The exact definition of 'very much worse' is of course arbitrary, but it can be precisely defined by a researcher. Rutter and Yule (1975) use the statistical criterion of 2 standard errors below prediction. The details of this criterion need not concern the reader who is not statistically minded, suffice to say that on statistical grounds we would expect that only about 2 per cent of children would be reading this far below expectation.

A specific example may help to clarify the use of multiple regression to define reading retardation. Imagine a child who is exactly 10 years old. An intelligence test shows that this child is somewhat above average for his age. We use the child's age and intelligence score to make a prediction of what we expect his reading level to be. Using the multiple regression procedure, we calculate that he would be expected to have a reading age of 10½; that is, reading like the average child who is 10½ years old. However, in actual fact the child is found to be reading at only the 7½ year old level. He is obviously reading far below the level we would expect for a child of his age and intelligence. If we define any child of this age who is reading more than 2½ years below the expected level as being a retarded reader, then this child will fall into that category.

Let us take one more example. Imagine another 10 year old child who is found to perform very poorly on an intelligence test. On the basis of this child's age and intelligence level, we expect that he would have a reading age of 8 years. In fact, the child is reading at the 7½ year old level – 6 months below expectation. Although this child is also a poor reader, he does not qualify as a specific reading retardate by our definition, because his reading performance is much less than 2½ years below expectation. Rather, this child would fit the category of general reading backwardness.

As mentioned previously, it would be expected on statistical grounds that roughly 2 per cent of children would be classified as retarded readers by Rutter and Yule's (1975) criterion. However, the actual incidence of specific reading retardation has been found to be much higher than this in a number of studies of English school children. I have found this same result myself with Australian school children. Figure 2.1 shows some results of this kind from two English epidemiological studies – one from the Isle of Wight on the southern coast of England and one in an inner London area. In both regions, the incidence of specific reading retardation is higher than expected. Normally, we would expect to find that extreme underachievement at reading is just as common as extreme achievement – in other words, that there are as many very good readers as there are very poor readers. However, the finding that the incidence of specific

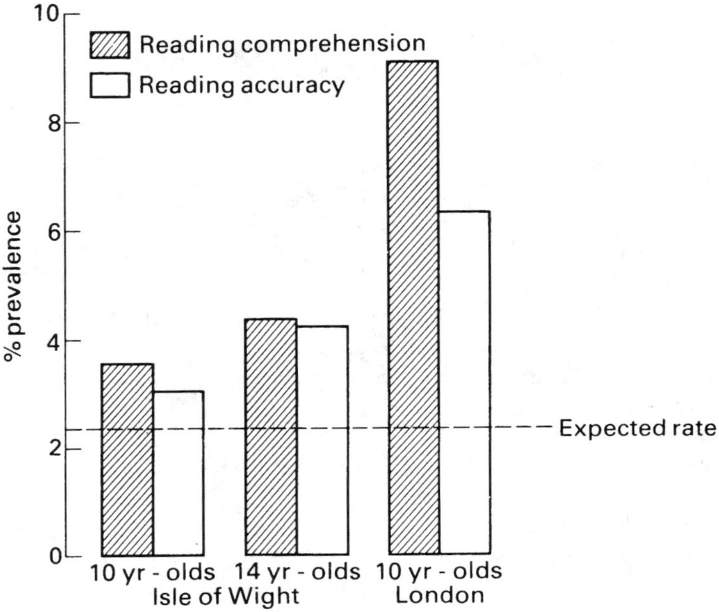

Figure 2.1 Observed and expected rates of specific reading retardation
Rutter & Yule, 1975

reading retardation is higher than expected indicates otherwise. Rutter and Yule (1975) have suggested that the higher than expected incidence of specific reading retardation indicates that this disability constitutes more than just the botton end of a continuum of reading achievement. In other words, it is possible that at least some of these children differ qualitatively from the rest of the population. To understand this argument it is worth considering the reasons for similarly high incidences at the bottom end of other human traits. For example, intelligence follows a similar pattern. On statistical grounds, we might expect that there are as many very intelligent people in the population as there are very unintelligent people. In point of fact, there are more mentally retarded people in the population than would be expected on statistical grounds. This is thought to reflect the occurrence of such factors as brain damage at birth and genetic disorders such as Down's Syndrome. By analogy, similar specific deficits might occur in the realm of reading aptitude and cause a higher than expected incidence of very poor reading achievement. One possibility is that there is an inherited predisposition to have difficulties in learning to read, as is implied by the concept of developmental dyslexia. However, the high incidence of specific reading retardation could also be produced by some qualitatively different environmental factor affecting some children. At present, we have no clear evidence which would allow us to choose either way.

Sex difference in incidence

Studies of poor readers referred to clinics have consistently found that males are seen much more frequently than females. This sex difference has been reported to hold in every country where it has been studied. Furthermore, it seems that this sex difference does not arise simply because of a greater tendency on the part of teachers and parents to refer boys to clinics. Epidemiological studies show a similar sex difference. For example, the Isle of Wight study found that 77 per cent of children with specific reading retardation were boys, and only 23 per cent were girls. With general reading backwardness, on the other hand, only 54 per cent of the children were found to be boys.

In the past, many people have suggested that this sex difference represented the operation of some genetic factor which manifests itself more commonly in males than in females. Such sex-linked genetic effects are certainly known in other spheres, such as colour blindness, where a specific gene manifests its effect in males more often than in females. However, at this stage, we have no evidence as to whether this sex difference in the incidence of specific reading retardation is due to genetic or environmental factors, or a combination of the two.

Social class difference

Although one might expect a tendency for children with specific reading retardation to come from the poorest sections of the community, the findings of the Isle of Wight study indicated that this is not the case. In that study, the children were placed into one of four social class categories on the basis of their father's occupation.

A Professional or managerial.
B Non-manual, clerical including minor supervisory grades.
C Skilled
D Semiskilled or unskilled.

Table 2.1 shows the social class distribution of normal children, children with intellectual retardation and children with specific reading retardation. Although intellectual retardation occurs more commonly in the lowest social class, this is not the case with specific reading retardation. In fact, there is practically no difference in the frequency of normal and retarded readers (23 per cent versus 24 per cent) in this social class. However, there is a notable scarcity of retarded readers amongst the highest social classes. Whereas 33 per cent of normal children have fathers in non-manual occupations, only 14 per cent of retarded readers do. Part of the reason for comparatively few retarded readers having fathers in non-manual occupations may be that these are the occupations in which reading is most crucial. If the fathers of retarded readers themselves tended to have reading problems, they might have difficulties in entering non-manual occupations. For this reason, they might more frequently tend towards skilled manual occupations where literacy skills are less important. In fact, there is evidence that a history of reading difficulties is often found in the families of children with specific reading retardation.

Table 2.1

Social class	Normal children %	Intellectual Retardation %	Specific reading retardation %
A	19	8	8
B	14	5	6
C	43	41	58
D	23	39	24
Unknown	1	7	3

Source: Adapted from Rutter, Tizard and Whitmore (1970), p. 114.

Family characteristics

It has been found in interviews with the parents of retarded readers that they often report a family history of reading or speech retardation. However, family histories of this sort are reported as commonly in cases of general reading backwardness as in specific reading retardation. Table 2.2 shows some of the results obtained from parental interviews in the Isle of Wight study. Although this study gave some interesting findings, interviews with parents are probably not the ideal basis for assessing whether a disorder has a family history. Parents whose children are having difficulties may have some bias towards reporting a family history of the disability. On the other hand, parents whose children are not having reading difficulties may fail to report family histories when they do occur. Nevertheless, there is reason to believe that the findings from parental interviews are reflecting a true association. A study by Finucci, Guthrie, Childs, Abbey and Childs (1976) on a clinic sample gave reading tests to the members of the immediate family of these children and found similar results. The use of objective reading tests rules out the possibility that there was some bias in reporting. Certainly, clinic samples may not be fully representative of retarded readers in general, but we can at least conclude that a family history of reading problems is characteristic of *some* retarded readers.

Another characteristic of the families of retarded readers is their size. In the Isle of Wight study, retarded readers tended to come from larger families than did normal readers. For example, 58 per

Table 2.2 Percentage of children showing family histories

Type of problem	Normal children %	General reading backwardness %	Specific reading retardation %
Family history of reading problems	9	36	34
Family history of speech delay	4	9	10

Source: Adapted from Rutter and Yule (1975), p. 188, and Rutter, Tizard and Whitmore (1970), p. 68.

cent of the retarded readers came from families with 4 or more children as against only 33 per cent for normal children. At the other end of the scale, a mere 5 per cent of retarded readers were only children compared with 11 per cent of normal readers.

Not only do retarded readers tend to come from large families, but there is also a slight tendency for them to be the later born children within a family. In other words, amongst retarded readers there are fewer children who are eldest in the family and more who are youngest in the family than would be expected. The reason for the association between large family size and a higher incidence of specific reading retardation may be that the parents of larger families spend less time directly helping their children academically and in stimulating the basic language skills on which the ability to read depends. Obviously, the parents of two children will have more time to spend with each child than will the parents of a family of five. Furthermore, parents will inevitably have more time to spend with a first-born child than with later ones. The eldest starts off life as an only child and can accordingly command much of his parents' time. Later children are born into a family where there are already competitors for the parents' intellectual stimulation. The youngest child is, of course, the worst off in this regard.

We would intuitively expect that parents who encourage their children's reading are less likely to have children with reading problems. In fact, there is evidence showing that parental involvement in reading is related to a child's reading achievement. A study by Hewison and Tizard (1980) looked at this relationship amongst 7-8-year-old children from a working class population in London. They found that a number of different aspects of a child's home environment are related to reading achievement, but the strongest factor to emerge was whether or not the mother regularly heard the child read. This factor was found to be much more important than whether the mother read to the child. Table 2.3 shows the percentage of children whose mothers listened to them read, classified according to whether they were above or below average in intelligence and reading achievement. These results show that children who are below average readers, irrespective of intelligence, are less likely to have mothers who listened to them read on a regular basis. Furthermore, Hewison and Tizard found that the greater amount of this type of coaching a mother gave her child, the higher her child's reading achievement was likely to be.

Table 2.3 Percentage of children whose mothers listened to them read

	Below average at reading %	Above average at reading %
Below Average Intelligence	18	69
Above Average Intelligence	24	86

Source: Adapted from Hewison and Tizard, 1980.

Community and school characteristics

We saw earlier that epidemiological studies in both the Isle of Wight and in an inner London area had shown a higher than expected incidence of specific reading retardation. However, perhaps even more notable was the large difference in the incidence of the disability between the two communities. Specific reading retardation is roughly twice as common amongst 10 year olds in London than amongst children of the same age on the Isle of Wight.

A study by Rutter, Yule, Quinton, Rowlands, Yule and Berger (1975) attempted to account for these community differences in terms of family and school influences. First of all, they examined the characteristics of those families *within* a particular community who had children with specific reading retardation. As we have already seen, such families tend to be larger than average and the father is less frequently employed in a higher status occupation. These researchers also examined the characteristics of those schools *within* a community which had a large number of children with specific reading retardation. They found that these schools had a higher teacher turnover as well as tendencies towards having high pupil turnover, higher absenteeism, a higher proportion of immigrant children, and a higher proportion of children receiving free meals. Having established which characteristics of families and schools were associated with specific reading retardation *within* a particular community, Rutter and his colleagues then looked at whether there was also a difference between the Isle of Wight and the inner London area in these characteristics. If there were such differences, this would help account for the big difference in the incidence of specific reading retardation between the two communities. They found that these differences did indeed exist. For example, the inner London area was found to have larger families than the Isle of Wight. Furthermore, inner London schools were found to have higher pupil and teacher turnover, higher absenteeism, a greater proportion of immigrant children, and a higher proportion of children receiving free meals. In short, the inner London area was characterised by the sort of social circumstances which had previously been shown to be associated with specific reading retardation.

In a more recent study, Rutter, Maugham, Mortimore and Ouston (1979) looked in greater detail at which characteristics of schools were associated with a greater incidence of academic and social problems. These researchers studied a total of 12 high schools in an inner London area. The schools were found to differ substantially in academic attainment (as measured by public examination results), level of attendance, children's behaviour in school, and delinquency. Rutter and colleagues attempted to find the characteristics of the schools which led to these differences in outcomes. Surprisingly, they found that the physical and administrative features of schools (e.g., class sizes, space available, age of buildings, administrative organisation) were not related to pupils' academic performance or social behaviour. However, certain characteristics of schools as social institutions were related to pupil outcome. Schools which produced greater academic gains tended to have the following social characteristics: greater stress was placed on the academic side of the school; teachers interacted with the whole class rather than with individual pupils; lessons seldom finished early; children's work was often displayed on the walls; there were general standards of classroom discipline expected for the whole school, rather than the standard of discipline being left to the individual teacher to decide; there were more school outings; pupils were more willing to consult teachers about personal problems; the school provided a pleasant and comfortable environment for the children to work in; a high proportion of pupils were given the opportunity of holding positions of responsibility; administrative decisions were made at senior staff level rather than in the staffroom; teachers felt that their point of view was taken into account when administrative decisions were made; and a check was put on whether teachers set homework. Another important factor was the balance of ability of a school's pupils. Schools which had a fair proportion of academically able students had better outcomes. It seems that the presence of a nucleus of able students had a positive influence on the other pupils in a school. In short, although this study was not concerned specifically with the incidence of reading retardation, it showed that differences between schools are related to pupil differences in academic performance.

Association with other problems

Although specific reading retardation is specific in the sense that general intelligence remains at a much higher level than reading achievement, this does not necessarily imply that reading is the only area of academic retardation in these children. In fact, deficiencies in other academic areas, and even in social behaviour, are frequently found. For example, it is well known that retarded readers are generally also retarded spellers and this was found to be the case with children on the Isle of Wight. Actually, specific reading retardates tended to be even further behind in spelling than in reading. Furthermore, these children also tended to be behind in arithmetic, although the degree of retardation was not as severe as for spelling or reading. One possible reason for retarded readers also having problems in spelling is that they have some sort of underlying cognitive deficit which affects both of these skills. Such a cognitive deficit might also produce the arithmetic deficit, but it is also possible that the arithmetic problem is a secondary consequence of the reading problem. Reading is such a fundamental academic skill that any reading retardation will have adverse effects on other academic subjects which require the use of reading. Even in arithmetic, problems are frequently presented in writing, and the child who cannot comprehend the written problem is at a grave disadvantage no matter how great his or her aptitude for mathematics might be.

Other problems that have often been linked to reading retardation are delinquency and emotional instability. Again, the Isle of Wight study confirms that these disorders are indeed sometimes related. In that study, parents and teachers were given questionnaires in which they had to indicate whether certain behavioral or emotional problems applied to a particular child. Some typical problems listed in these questionnaires were:

> Very restless, often running about or jumping up and down.
> Hardly ever still.
> Tends to do things on his own — rather solitary.
> Irritable. Is quick to 'fly off the handle'.
> Bullies other children.

Often tells lies.
Frequently fights with other children.

Children who, according to either parents or teachers, had a large number of such problems were regarded as having a psychiatric disorder. Where possible, these children were divided into two broad groups — antisocial or neurotic — according to the predominant types of problems they had.
Antisocial children were characterised by descriptions like *truants, destructive, fights, disobedient, lies, steals, bullies;* while neurotic children were given such descriptions as *worried, miserable, fearful, fussy, school tears, absent from school for trivial reasons.* In addition to the parent and teacher questionnaires, each child was interviewed by a child psychiatrist who designated him or her as either psychiatrically normal or abnormal.

On all measures, children with specific reading retardation were found to have a greater incidence of psychiatric disorder. For example, on the parental questionnaire, 24 per cent of the retarded readers were classified as having some sort of psychiatric disturbance as against only 8 per cent of normal readers. A similar difference was found on the teacher's questionnaire (37 per cent versus 10 per cent) as well as with the psychiatric interview (8 per cent versus 1 per cent). When the children were looked at in terms of the category of their disorder (neurotic or antisocial), it was found that the retarded readers more often had disorders of the antisocial type than the neurotic type. It might be thought that this association simply reflects the greater number of boys who are retarded readers, since boys tend to engage in antisocial behavior more than girls. However, this finding holds up even when the sex difference is allowed for.

An interesting question to ask is whether the increased incidence of antisocial behaviour in retarded readers is a cause or an effect of their reading problems. Both possibilities seem plausible. For example, we could imagine that a child who engages in antisocial behaviour when he starts school would fail to gain as much from reading instruction as other children, even if he were quite intelligent. Alternatively, it is possible that a child who fails to progress in reading at the rate of other children might develop antisocial behaviours as a reaction to failure. Yet another possibility is that antisocial behaviour and reading retardation are associated because they are both caused by a third factor such as the child's family circumstances. These various possibilities are diagrammed in Figure 2.2. One way

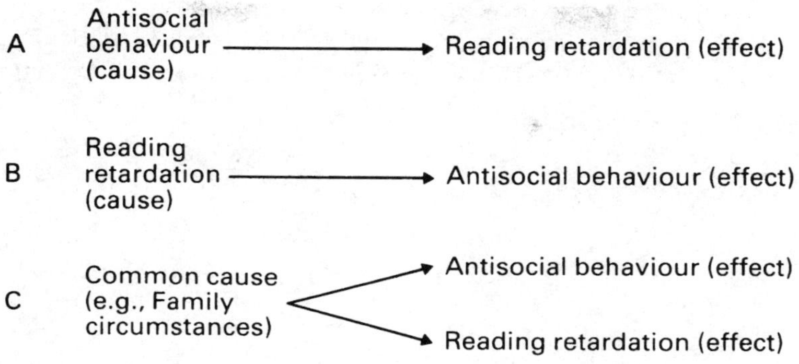

Figure 2.2 Possible causative relationships linking reading retardation to antisocial behaviour

of testing these various alternatives is to study the antisocial behaviour of children before they even start school and follow them through several years of school to see whether those with antisocial tendencies develop a higher incidence of reading retardation than other children. If these children do more often become retarded readers, then it is fair to conclude that antisocial behaviour leads to reading problems.

On the other hand, if children become antisocial as a consequence of their reading problems, we should find that retarded readers become increasingly antisocial as they progress through the early years of school. A study by McMichael (1979) has attempted to sort out the relationship between reading retardation and antisocial behaviour using this sort of approach. She found that children who exhibited antisocial behaviour at the start of their schooling tended to be poorer at reading after completing two years of school. This finding indicates that reading difficulties can be a consequence of antisocial behaviour. However, McMichael also found that these antisocial children performed poorly on a reading readiness test given at the time they started school. In other words, these children tended to lack certain skills essential for learning to read. On the other issue of whether reading difficulties produce emotional problems as a secondary consequence, McMichael's evidence was negative. However, she may not have followed the children's progress for a sufficiently long period to detect the emotional consequences of reading failure. It would be most surprising indeed if reading retardation did not produce some secondary consequences by the end of primary schooling.

Long-term prospects

Although it would be nice to think that retarded readers are simply late-bloomers who will eventually catch up with their peers, the evidence unfortunately indicates otherwise. Without remedial help, these children continue to have academic problems later on. Yule (1973) was able to follow up over 90 per cent of the Isle of Wight poor readers, four to five years after they had been originally studied. He tested these children again on intelligence, reading, spelling, and arithmetic. Yule found that the children with specific reading retardation, as well as those with general reading backwardness, were still far behind in all academic subjects. However, perhaps the most startling finding was that the children with specific reading retardation had made *less* progress in reading and spelling than had the children with general reading backwardness. The surprising aspect of this finding is that children with specific reading retardation are more intelligent than those with general reading backwardness. In other words, the more intelligent children were showing slower progress in reading and spelling. Exactly the opposite pattern was found for progress in arithmetic. In this subject, the children with specific reading retardation generally made greater progress than the children with general reading backwardness. This unusual pattern of results seems to support the validity of making a distinction between children who are specifically retarded in reading and children who are generally backward. The pattern of achievement gains indicates that there may be some difference between the deficits of these two groups of children. Unfortunately, Yule gave no indication of what had happened to the children at school in the intervening years. For example, we do not know which children received remediation, and in what areas. There may have been some differences between the retarded and backward readers in the frequency with which they received such help.

Less is known about the prospects for retarded readers after they leave school. Although several studies have looked into the adult outcomes of retarded readers who were referred to clinics as children, these have not produced consistent results (Herjanic and Penick, 1972). Some studies find that retarded readers still have reading and spelling problems in adulthood and that they are more likely to be in lower-status occupations, but other studies do not support these findings. The conflicting evidence on this issue simply attests to the problems in drawing any general conclusions from clinic samples. So often, the children referred to clinics are atypical of the general population of retarded readers, and there may even be differences between the characteristics of one clinic sample and another. A clear answer will only emerge when total populations of retarded readers are followed through to adulthood.

3 Specific reading retardation: The nature of the reading deficit

Views of the reading process

Before looking at what goes wrong with the reading process in children who are having difficulties, we need first of all to know something about how reading works in the person who reads well. I will refer to such people as *skilled readers*.

About a decade ago, researchers interested in reading could be broadly divided into two camps according to their general view of how skilled reading took place. In one camp were those who viewed reading as a *bottom-up* process. According to the bottom-up viewpoint, the reader would process a written passage as a series of steps such as the following:

1 The reader moves his eye to the first portion of the printed page.

2 The visual system analyses the first word of the page letter by letter.

3 Each letter is converted into sound, so that the reader ends up working out the pronunciation of the word.

4 The pronunciation of the word gives access to its meaning which is stored in the reader's memory.

5 Subsequent words are similarly analysed until a whole phrase has been completed and the meaning of this phrase can be worked out.

It is not hard to see why this view of reading is described as bottom-up. The reader is viewed as starting at the bottom – identify letters – and working up to higher and higher levels until ultimately the meaning of the passage has been worked out. This view of reading seems quite ordered and logical and will no doubt be quite appealing to somebody who is thinking about reading for the first time. However, as we shall see, there are reasons for dismissing it as a plausible view of reading.

Let us at this point take a look at the opposite point of view which sees reading as a *top-down* process. According to the top-down view, the reader is guided primarily by his expectations about what is on the printed page. That is, the reader uses his knowledge of the world, his knowledge of language, and his knowledge of print to anticipate what information lies on the page being read. These anticipations guide the reader to sample information from the page which either confirms or disconfirms them. Rather than the reader proceeding letter-by-letter and word-by-word, as in the bottom-up view, he is held to select out only the information relevant to his anticipations.

The following passage taken from Goodman (1967) illustrates perfectly the top-down position:

> Reading is a selective process. It involves partial use of available minimal language cues selected from perceptual input on the basis of the reader's expectations. As this partial information is processed, tentative decisions are made to be confirmed, rejected, or refined as reading progresses (pp. 126-7).

Another well-known proponent of the top-down view is Frank Smith (1978) who writes:

> Readers do not normally attend to print with their minds blank, with no prior purpose and with no expectation of what they might find in the text. Readers normally look for meaning rather than strive to identify letters or words. The way readers look for meaning is not to consider all possibilities nor to make reckless guesses about just one, but rather they predict within the most likely range of alternatives (p. 163).

In short, the top-down view sees the reader's anticipations, which are based on his knowledge of language, as acting downwards to guide processing of the printed page.

Lest the reader is wondering why a top-down view would be proposed as an alternative to a bottom-up view, try reading the following two passages aloud as fast as possible. The important point to note is the time taken for each of the passages.

1 one-fifteenth that uninhabitable difference USA states about

1 United population fraction roughly the of being area its There 220 over the in million against as only is Australian major one States the of that United means this of density population the Australia in much of with Australia desert is country dry contiguous the area 48 of the Australia has same the although a has it only about only vast this to a factor very contributing as are inhabitants States virtually.
2 Although Australia has roughly the same area as the forty-eight contiguous states of the USA, it has only a fraction of the population. There are only about 14 million inhabitants in Australia, as against over 220 million in the United States. This means that the population density of Australia is only about one-fifteenth that of the United States. One major factor contributing to this vast difference is that Australia is a very dry country, with much of its area being virtually uninhabitable desert.

No doubt you read the second passage much quicker than the first even though they contain exactly the same words. Consider why this was the case. When you read the scrambled passage you were forced to read as the bottom-up viewpoint would suggest – word by word. You were not able to use your general knowledge of the world and your knowledge of language to anticipate what was coming next in the passage, so your reading was slow and laboured. However, you read the normal passage much faster because knowledge from the 'top' was able to influence your processing of the print.

Although the. top-down view of reading has provided a useful counter to the rather simplistic bottom-up view, it may be inadequate in some ways itself. One argument against the top-down view is that it would be very inefficient for someone to read purely by this process. Constantly generating anticipations and testing them against the printed page seems a very inefficient way to read when it is possible to process the print directly. The top-down view assumes that it is quicker for a reader to proceed by generating anticipations about what is on the printed page than to attempt to recognise words on a purely visual basis. However, this assumption is difficult to support and has been questioned by a number of researchers.

More recently, a third view has been put forward which gives a more adequate account of skilled reading than its predecessors and, to some extent, incorporates the best features of each. This is the *interactive* view, which holds that both bottom-up and top-down processes are going on simultaneously. According to the interactive view, information from the printed page is processed bottom-up starting at letters, then words, clause meanings, and so on. However, the reader also has expectations which act downwards towards lower levels. Thus, current expectations about the meaning of the clause being analysed influence the processing at the lower word level and, similarly, current expectations about the word which is being identified influence the processing at the lower letter level. The interactive view and the top-down view are similar in that both see the reader's expectations as acting downwards to influence the processing of the printed page. However, the interactive view differs in that it sees expectations as arising, not solely at the highest level of language comprehension, but also at lower levels such as word and letter identification.

The distinctions between these various views of skilled reading might appear rather abstract, so an analogy might be of some help in explaining the differences. An appropriate analogy would involve the strategies used by a person travelling a complex but unfamiliar route between two cities. Such a traveller might adopt different strategies somewhat analogous to the strategies implied by the bottom-up, top-down, and interactive views of reading.

A bottom-up strategy of finding the route between the cities would be to follow the signposts along the way. Using this strategy, our traveller would start off at City A in the direction indicated by the first signpost. When a new signpost was encountered, the traveller would reorient his direction accordingly. Provided the route was adequately signposted, the traveller would eventually reach City B. We could say that this traveller was adopting a bottom-up strategy because he was directing himself completely by information provided along the route. In this sense, he is somewhat similar to a reader whose reading is completely directed by what is on the printed page.

A second strategy our traveller could adopt is to rely on a map to guide his journey. Following this strategy, the traveller would set off from City A using the map to tell him the right direction. From his reading of the map, the traveller might expect that he has to travel two blocks and turn right, then after crossing a bridge turn left, then travel a long distance until he comes across a five-way intersection, and so on. In other words, the map would give the traveller certain definite expectations about what he might encounter on his journey. Rather than look out for all the signposts, our traveller would be selectively looking for the particular features that his map told him were important. His attention to what he saw along the way would therefore be totally directed towards confirming the predictions he had made from reading the map. This traveller's strategy might be called a top-down one because he is being guided by a map which is directing his attention to features of the route he is travelling. In this way, the traveller is like a reader whose knowledge of language directs him to selectively process the printed page.

The interactive traveller's strategy should by now be obvious. This type of traveller would be guided by both signposts and map with each source of knowledge producing expectations about the other. For example, from reading the map the traveller might expect to cross a bridge soon after making a particular left-hand turn. This expectation might lead the traveller to look out for signs concerning bridges. This is an example of a top-down influence, with the map influencing the traveller to look out for certain signs. Conversely, there would be bottom-up influences when a signpost influences the traveller to have expectations about what is on the map. For example, imagine that the traveller comes across a sign saying RAILWAY CROSSING AHEAD and this influences him to look at the map to confirm whether such a crossing is marked where he thinks it should be. Probably most people would agree that they adopt such an interactive strategy when travelling a complex route and, as we have seen, the processes involved in skilled reading are also most appropriately described as interactive.

A major purpose of initially introducing you to these broad overviews of skilled reading is to provide a sort of antidote for what follows. When studying a complex psychological process such as reading, it is inevitably easier to deal with it in terms of small components rather than as the interactive process it really is. For example, we know that retarded readers are poor at reading, but we need to know whether they have problems with the whole process or only with specific parts of it. To answer questions of this sort, we have to look at reading in a piecemeal fashion, one part at a time. Of course, the danger of carving up such a complex process is that we can easily lose sight of the complex interrelations amongst the parts. Now, having received this forewarning, let us proceed to look at specific reading retardation in terms of how adequately different components of the reading process are functioning.

At the end of the chapter we will return to the interactive view of reading and look at how the retarded reader's strengths and weaknesses in various subcomponents of reading interrelate together to produce some surprising effects on the overall process.

Paths to Word Meaning

The ultimate purpose of reading is to ascertain the meaning of the text being read. An important stage in achieving this goal is the identification of the meanings of individual words. This is not to imply that we read by identifying the meanings of each word in a text, one at a time. However, identification of word meanings must play some important role in skilled reading. Many psychologists like to think of the meanings of words as being stored in a sort of mental dictionary – often referred to as the *mental lexicon*. However, the entries in the mental lexicon are not arranged alphabetically as they are in the sort of dictionaries with which we are familiar. Just how the entries in this mental lexicon are organised is still a hotly debated issue, but one which need not concern us here. What is more interesting for present purposes is the manner in which the reader uses the information from the printed page to access the entry in the lexicon where the meaning of a word is stored. There are essentially two mechanisms by which an entry to the mental lexicon can be accessed. The first is to use the visual pattern of the word being read to derive a visual representation, or code, which is then used to find the entry in the lexicon. Teachers often refer to this process as *whole-word* or *sight-word* reading. We can diagram this process as a series of boxes and arrows, where each box represents a stage of mental processing, and the arrows show how information is transferred from one stage to the next:

A second mechanism is to use the visual information from the printed word to derive its pronunciation, perhaps using some sort of rules for relating letters to their sounds, and then using the pronunciation to access the meaning in the mental lexicon. Teachers might refer to this process as reading by *phonics*. Of course, there is no implication that this type of reading necessarily involves pronouncing a word out loud. What we are talking about is simply a mental representation of the pronunciation. I will refer to this sort of inner speech as a *phonological code.* The process involved can be diagrammed as follows:

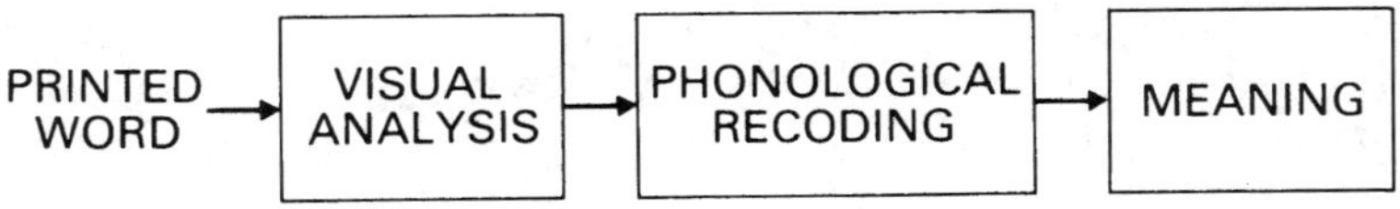

These two ways of accessing an appropriate entry in the lexicon are not, in fact, contradictory. Both can be used and are used at different times. For example, if we come across a printed word we have never seen before, we are forced to access its meaning by converting it into a phonological code. On the other hand, we have no choice but to access meaning directly from a visual code when we read symbols such as &, $, 8, and abbreviations such as kg., sq., and etc. Although these are extreme cases, there is evidence to support the existence of both pathways to meaning in reading more typical words. Some researchers believe that the two ways of accessing meaning go on in parallel with each other when we read any word. It is as though the two paths are having a sort of race to access the entry in the mental lexicon. We can diagram this *race model* as follows:

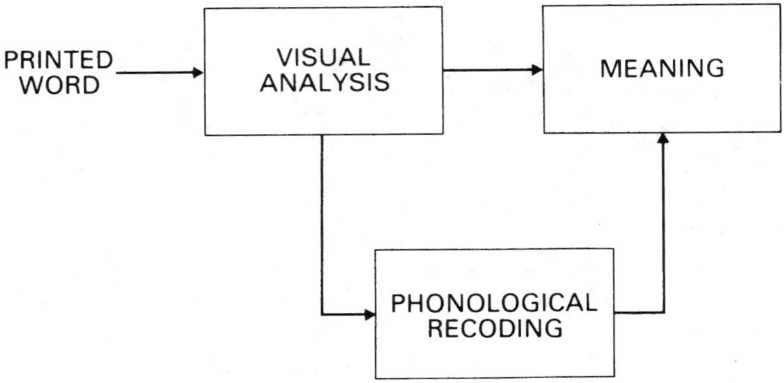

In skilled reading, the direct path using the visual code is faster and will be first to reach the entry in the mental lexicon. However, in instances where a printed word is unfamiliar, the phonological pathway will win. An example might be in reading a word such as *gralloch* which is very rare. Because of its unfamiliarity, even a skilled reader will fail to identify the word by the direct visual pathway and so the phonological pathway will win the race. From this example, you should be able to see that beginning readers must rely much more on the phonological pathway for word identification, because so few words are visually familiar to them. As they get older and have more practice at reading, children are able to identify more and more printed words by the visual pathway, so the importance of the phonological pathway declines.

Word identification by retarded readers

Having distinguished the two paths to word identification, let us now look at the performance of retarded readers with each of them. To begin with, we will look at the evidence concerning the phonological pathway.

As we have seen, the phonological pathway is used for reading unfamiliar words, so the ability to work out pronunciations for words of this type is a good measure of how well the phonological pathway is functioning. Unfortunately, it is generally not possible to know whether or not a particular word is unfamiliar to a given reader. A way around this problem is to make up artificial words which, although they look like plausible English words, happen not to be. Words of this type are often referred to as *nonsense words*. Sample nonsense words are: *blen, ab, ind, porsun, theld*. Skilled readers seldom have any difficulty in producing pronunciations for printed nonsense words of this type and even show high agreement as to what they consider the 'correct' pronunciation to be even though there is strictly no correct pronunciation.

Using this method of assessing the phonological pathway, Firth (1972) tested a large number of 8-year old Australian school children who were either average or poor readers. He divided these good and poor readers into two groups – those of average intelligence and those of low intelligence. As a result he had two groups of poor readers – those with specific reading retardation and those with general reading backwardness.

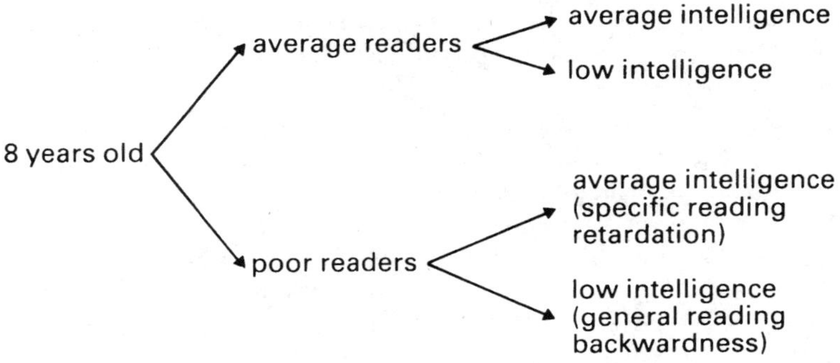

Firth gave these children a list of 170 nonsense words to read aloud and found a dramatic difference in performance between the good and poor readers. The average number of nonsense words read correctly by each group is shown in Table 3.1. As you can see, both groups of poor readers did very badly indeed. Firth described the performance of the typical poor reader at this task as follows:

> The average readers sailed through the nonsense word test very rapidly, sometimes so fast that it was difficult to keep pace in recording answers. Usually they did not 'sound out' these unfamiliar words, but pronounced them without hesitation. The bad readers, by contrast, found the task very difficult. The errors made by the bad readers were usually failures to produce any pronunciation at all, rather than the production of incorrect pronunciations. The worst of the bad readers, although able to read a few Schonell R1 words, could not produce any pronunciation at all for these nonsense words. Even with explanations, examples, coaching, and sounding of some letters by the tester,

Table 3.1 Average number of nonsense words read correctly

	Average intelligence	Low intelligence
Average readers	118	119
Poor readers	35	18

> they still found the task impossible. The best of the bad readers had some idea of what phonics was about, and could produce some correct pronunciations. However, these pronunciations were produced very slowly and laboriously and with much sounding out of the letters (pp. 123-4).

Even when retarded readers can correctly work out the pronunciation of a nonsense word, they tend to be much slower at doing so than normal readers. The slowness of working out a pronunciation can be accurately measured by presenting a printed word on a screen and simultaneously starting up a clock. When the reader responds with a pronunciation, it is detected by a microphone which sends a signal to stop the clock. The clock has then recorded the time taken to begin a pronunciation after the word has been presented. Using this technique, Seymour and Porpodas (1980) have shown that retarded readers are much slower at reading nonsense words aloud, even when they can do it correctly. They found that the more letters a word has, the slower the retarded readers are at reading it compared to normal readers.

Other research, by Snowling (1980), has shown that retarded readers have problems in reading nonsense words even when they do not have to pronounce them out loud. What she did was to show children a printed nonsense word and then give a pronunciation straight afterwards, which could be either right or wrong. The child had to put a tick on a sheet of paper if the pronunciation was right and a cross if it was wrong. For example, a child might be shown the printed nonsense word SOND, then the tester would say 'sond', and the child should make a tick on his or her piece of paper. To take a different example, the tester might show SINT, then say 'snit', and the child should respond with a cross. Basically, this task required the children to recode the printed nonsense word into inner speech, hold this pronunciation in memory, and then compare it to the pronunciation provided by the tester. Snowling found that retarded readers generally performed much more poorly than normal readers on this version of the nonsense word reading task. Furthermore, Snowling took her analysis one step further. She compared the performance of the retarded readers to that of good readers who had the same overall reading ability. This comparison is best explained by a specific example. Imagine we have some 10-year-old children who are reading at the level of 8-year-olds. We then compare the performance of these children with that of 8-year-olds who are reading at their own age level. Although the 10-year-olds are retarded readers and the 8-year-olds are average readers, the overall reading achievement of the two groups is the same. Snowling found that retarded readers perform more poorly at nonsense word reading even when compared to younger children in this way. At first glance, this result seems quite paradoxical: we have two groups of children who are equal in reading achievement and yet one group is worse at reading nonsense words. However, this result can be explained by considering the different ways in which the older retarded and younger average readers achieved their equivalent reading levels. The retarded readers may have been able to identify a large number of words without the use of phonological recoding. In other words, because they were older and would probably have had more experience at reading, they had built up a larger sight-word vocabulary which partly offset their relative disadvantage with phonological recoding. Snowling also found that the retarded readers did not get better at reading nonsense words as their reading achievement increased. For example, retarded readers who were reading at the 7-year-old level tended to perform no differently from retarded readers who were reading at the 10-year-old level. With normal readers, on the other hand, increases in reading achievement were accompanied by increases in the ability to read the nonsense words. It therefore appears that the retarded readers were increasing their reading skills as they got older purely by building up a larger sight-word vocabulary. Snowling's findings seem to imply that retarded readers fare rather better at identifying words by the direct visual pathway than by the phonological pathway. Let us now turn to some more direct evidence on this issue.

Earlier in the chapter we saw that there are certain symbols used in English like *$*, *&*, and %, whose meaning must be found by a purely visual pathway. Such symbols contain no clues as to how they are pronounced, so any reader who came across one of them for the first time could not work out its meaning. He or she would have to rely on the help of somebody else to decipher it. Although this way of representing meaning by a visual symbol is only rarely used in English and the other European languages, it forms the basis of one of the world's major writing systems – Chinese. Chinese characters do not represent sound directly as our English alphabet does. Rather, Chinese characters represent meanings directly. We could fairly say that Chinese characters are always identified by the direct visual pathway and never by the phonological pathway.*

Therefore, the ability to learn the meanings of Chinese characters might be regarded as a measure of a child's aptitude for learning to identify words by the direct visual route.

A rather interesting demonstration that poor readers could learn to identify Chinese cnaracters adequately was carried out in the USA by Rozin, Poritsky and Sotsky (1971). They located a group of 8 black children in the second grade of an inner-city school who were doing very poorly at reading. These children were unable to read simple nonsense words like ZIF, WAT, and REN, and could not reliably read a set of rhyming words like CAT, FAT, MAT and SAT after being given the pronunciation of AT. Obviously these children had not managed to learn to identify words using the phonological pathway. Rozin and his colleagues attempted to teach these children to read the English equivalents of Chinese characters. Because the Chinese writing system represents meanings rather than sounds, it is quite possible to learn to read Chinese characters without knowing how to speak Chinese. The children were seen individually a few times each week and were tutored at reading Chinese characters as well as at normal English reading. Altogether, the children were tutored for a total of 8 to 14 hours each. During this time they were taught 30 Chinese characters which had been specially selected because they could be fitted together to make a large variety of meaningful sentences. The children learned the Chinese characters quite rapidly and were eventually able to read sentences and stories made up from them. Some of the sentences they could read are shown in Figure 3.1. Although these children had failed to learn the basics of phonological recoding after two years of schooling, they were able to read sentences of Chinese characters after a few hours tutoring. This study provides a dramatic demonstration that children with reading problems found it much easier to identify words by the direct visual pathway than by the phonological pathway. However, the study was simply a demonstration and not a controlled scientific experiment in any sense.

Other researchers have attempted to use more controlled experimental procedures to assess retarded readers' ability to identify words by the direct visual pathway. For example, I carried out an

*Actually, it is not quite as simple as this, because Chinese characters sometimes contain 'clues' to pronunciation.

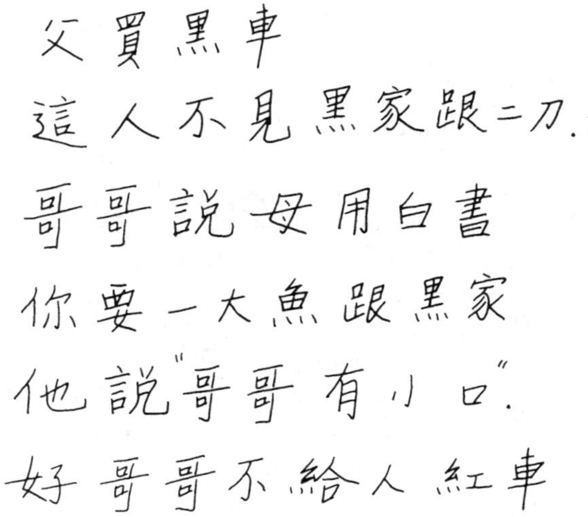
父買黑車
這人不見黑家跟二刀.
哥哥說母用白書
你要一大魚跟黑家
他說"哥哥有小口".
好哥哥不給人紅車

Sentences used in a final test of the acquisition of Chinese characters. The sentences read: 'Father buys black car. This man doesn't (not) see black house and two knives. Brother says mother uses white book. You want one big fish and black house. He says 'brother has small mouth'. Good brother doesn't (not) give man red car.' Eight children made an average of three errors on these 40 characters.

Figure 3.1
Source: From Rozin, Poritsky and Sotsky (1971).

experiment in which retarded readers were compared to normal readers in their ability to associate meanings with word-like squiggles (Jorm, 1977b). Examples of these squiggles are shown in Figure 3.2. These squiggles are like the Chinese characters used by Rozin, Poritsky and Sotsky in that they must be identified by the direct visual pathway. The squiggles cannot be identified by phonological recoding because they do not provide any information about pronunciation. The word-like squiggles were printed on individual cards and shown to the children one at a time. As each squiggle was presented, the child was told that it said a certain word. After a child had been told what all the squiggles said, he or she was shown each one of them and asked to remember what it said. This sort of

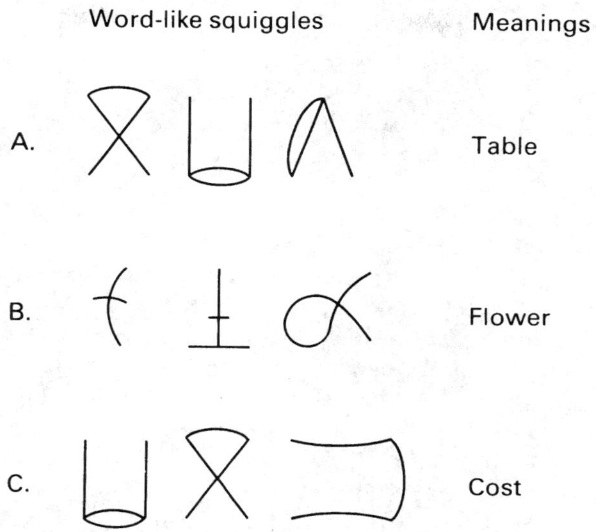

Figure 3.2 Examples of word-like squiggles together with their meanings
Source: Adapted from Jorm, 1977b.

procedure was repeated four times to give the children an opportunity to learn to identify the squiggles. To assess how much they had learned, a total was made of the number of times they could correctly identify a squiggle. It was found that the retarded readers learned just as much as the normal readers. Other researchers have found exactly the same results using similar tasks. It therefore seems that retarded readers are not deficient in the ability to associate meaningful spoken words with visual patterns.

Our conclusion so far is that retarded readers have problems in identifying printed words using the phonological pathway but not the direct visual pathway. The obvious question to ask at this point is: Why do these children have reading problems when they can learn to identify printed words using their direct visual pathways? After all, Chinese children learn to read quite adequately using this pathway alone, so we know it is possible. Why can't retarded readers treat printed English words just as if they were Chinese characters? To answer this question we need to consider in greater detail the role that phonological recoding plays for the beginning reader.

Recall that this pathway allows the child to work out unfamiliar words which may never have been encountered before. In fact, the fundamental advantage of an alphabetic writing system over the Chinese character system is that it allows the reader to work out unfamiliar words. A child learning to read Chinese characters will have great difficulty doing this and will often have to rely on a more skilled reader for help in such situations. In other words, phonological recoding allows the beginning reader to teach himself – an advantage which the direct visual pathway does not have. If children can master the rules of print-to-sound conversion during the early years of reading instruction, they are then able to teach themselves to identify new words later on. However, children who fail to master the principles of print-to-sound conversion will have to rely on teachers and parents to help them learn new words. Put another way, the direct visual pathway may depend largely on the phonological pathway for building up its capabilities. After an unfamiliar printed word has been worked out on a few occasions using phonological recoding, a child will learn to identify it by the more direct visual pathway. So what we find with retarded readers is that they are quite capable of identifying words using the direct visual pathway, but unable to do so with many words because their deficient phonological pathway has failed to help them build up an adequate sight-word vocabulary.

Comprehension in retarded readers

Identifying individual words is certainly an important component of the reading process. However, reading consists of more than the identification of isolated words. Usually, people read phrases, sentences, paragraphs, or complete texts and the meaning of what they read is more than the meaning of the individual words involved. Let us take the following two sentences as examples:

1 Did you know that dingoes sometimes kill sheep?
2 Did you know that sheep sometimes kill dingoes?

Although the individual words in these two sentences are identical, the meanings of the sentences are quite different. In other words, the meaning of a sentence is more than the sum of the meanings of the words which make it up. There are relations between the words of the sentence which are signalled by word order. There must be some quite complex mental processes which integrate the individual words in order to work out the meaning of the sentences. The nature of this comprehension process is dealt with in detail in a later chapter. The important question at this stage is whether retarded readers have any other deficiency beyond that at word identification. Obviously, problems in identifying the component words in a text will lead to poor comprehension, but how well will a retarded reader comprehend in situations where all the component words can be identified?

Some research by Guthrie (1973) suggests that retarded readers generally do have an additional comprehension deficit of this sort. Guthrie's study used a rather interesting method of assessing comprehension ability independently of word identification skills. Guthrie selected a group of retarded readers who were around 10 years old but whose word identification performance was only at the Grade 2 level. He then selected two groups of normal readers. One group consisted of children who were also around 10-years-old, but whose word identification performance was at the Grade 6 level. The second group of normal readers was made up of 7-year-olds whose word identification performance was at the expected Grade 2 level. In other words, one group of normal readers was equivalent to the retarded readers in age, but superior at word identification, while the other group was younger than the retarded readers but equal to them at word identification. Table 3.2 summarises the characteristics of the three groups of children in Guthrie's study. By

Table 3.2 Characteristics of the three groups of children in Guthrie's (1973) study

Group	Average age in years	Word identification: grade level
Retarded readers	10	2
Old normal readers	10	6
Young normal readers	7	2

comparing the reading comprehension of the retarded readers to that of the young normal readers, Guthrie was able to assess whether they have any comprehension deficit over and above that contributed by word identification problems. Both the young normal readers and the retarded readers had the same word identification ability, so if the retarded readers could not comprehend text as well as the young readers they must be deficient at some other component of the reading process. To assess these children's comprehension, Guthrie gave them what he called a *maze task*. The children had to silently read through passages which appeared as follows:

	horses		had
Both	flowers lifted their ears.	They	were heard the forest
	talk		some

	blanket.		on
ranger's	kept.	They are ready to go	before a trip.
	voice.		turned

As you can see, at certain points in the passages there are three alternative words provided but only one of these adequately fits the context. As the children read through such passages they had to circle the appropriate word whenever a set of alternatives was presented. The number of alternatives correctly circled gave a measure of comprehension. Using this measure, Guthrie found that the older normal readers comprehended the most, which was hardly surprising given their superior word identification skills. However, the young normal readers were found to comprehend better than the retarded readers, even though the two groups had equivalent word identification skills. This finding shows that retarded readers must have a comprehension deficit as well as a word identification deficit. However, Guthrie's study gave no real clue as to the nature of this comprehension deficit. Although he examined the types of errors made by the different groups of children, Guthrie found that the retarded readers tended to make the same sorts of mistakes as the normal readers. The retarded readers simply made more errors generally, rather than more errors of a specific sort. In the next chapter, we will gain further clues to the nature of this comprehension deficit when we look at the basic cognitive processing deficiencies characteristic of retarded readers. We will see that there may be a common factor behind both their phonological recoding problems and their comprehension deficit.

The interactive reading process in retarded readers

At the beginning of this chapter we looked at three overall views of the reading process – bottom-up, top-down, and interactive – and concluded that an interactive view seems to give the most reasonable account of skilled reading. We then looked at the reading process of retarded readers by breaking it into component parts. We saw that retarded readers often have a severe deficit at word identification via phonological recoding as well as an additional deficit in comprehension. We will now try to put the component parts back together again and look at how deficits in the components affect the overall interactive reading process.

Recall that the essence of the interactive view of reading is that high-level processes constrain low-level processes and, as well, low-level processes constrain high-level ones. Stanovich (1980) has pointed out an interesting implication of the interactive view; namely, that normal processes at one level can compensate for deficient processes at another level. For example, if somebody were poor at the low-level skill of word identification, they would rely more heavily on high-level factors such as sentence context. Conversely, if somebody were deficient at the high-level skill of generating expectations from context, then their reading would rely more heavily on the low-level skill of accurate word identification. Stanovich refers to this notion of a normal component of the reading process making up for a deficient one as the *compensatory hypothesis*. The compensatory hypothesis can be explained more clearly by harking back to our earlier analogy between reading and travelling a complex but unfamiliar route. Imagine that our traveller is setting out on his journey between City A and City B and has both a map and signposts to guide him. However, all the signposts are being repainted on the day of the journey, so none can be fully read. In this situation, the traveller would compensate for the deficient signposts by relying more heavily on the map than he otherwise would. Conversely, imagine that the map has had some ink spilt on it so that major portions are obliterated. The traveller would then have to rely on the signposts to find his way. In other words, the traveller compensates for any deficient source of information by relying more heavily on his intact source of information.

The nature of the reading deficit

We have seen that retarded readers often have a deficient sight-word vocabulary because of problems in using phonological recoding to help them learn new words. In other words, they are often unable to identify printed words using the direct visual pathway. However, in typical reading situations, the surrounding sentence context, as well as the visual features of a word, play a role in its identification. In fact, in certain very familiar contexts, we can correctly identify a word completely without the use of visual information. For example:

Make hay while the _______shines.

According to the compensatory hypothesis, a reader will rely more heavily on such high-level context cues if there is some difficulty in identifying words from low-level visual cues. This type of compensation can even be observed in skilled readers when the visual features of a word are not clearly discriminable, as in reading barely legible handwriting. In retarded readers, who have constant problems with word identification, the use of context cues should become especially important. Stanovich argues that retarded readers do indeed tend to compensate in this way and he cites results from several studies which indicate that this is the case. In some ways, the finding that retarded readers make greater use of context to aid word identification is surprising because, as we have seen, they are generally poorer at comprehension as well as poorer at word identification. In order to generate reasonable expectations about a printed word from surrounding context, a reader needs to be able to comprehend what he is reading at a satisfactory level. Indeed, it has often been found that retarded readers are poorer at predicting a missing word on the basis of the preceding context, as they were in Guthrie's (1973) maze task. However, there is a crucial difference between *being able to* predict from context and actually *making use of* this capability. Although normal readers can make better predictions from context, they make less use of this skill in word identification. The reason that normal readers rely less on context is that they do not have the same need for it because they can identify words quite well on the basis of their visual features.

Let us look at just one experiment which shows the compensatory mechanism operating in retarded readers. This particular experiment comes from a study by Perfetti, Goldman, and Hogaboam (1979) which involved fifth-grade students who were either retarded or normal readers. These children were timed for how long it took them to work out the pronunciations of printed words. In one part of the experiment the words were read in isolation, while in a second part of the experiment the words were read as part of a story. When words were presented in isolation, the children had to rely completely on low-level word identification skills. However, when the words were in a story context predictions derived from the preceding meaning could be used to aid word identification. It was found that both normal and retarded readers read words aloud faster when they were in a story context. However, the retarded readers gained more benefit from the story context than the normal readers. They improved their reading time from an average of 1.14 seconds per word in isolation to .82 seconds per word in context. For the normal readers, on the other hand, the improvement was from .74 seconds per word in isolation to .64 seconds per word in context. The greater benefit which the retarded readers received from the story context shows that they were relying more heavily on high-level context cues in reading the words. According to the compensatory hypothesis, this effect occurs because the retarded reader needs to compensate for deficiencies in their low-level word identification skills. Another interesting feature of this experiment is that Perfetti, Goldman, and Hogaboam assessed the children's ability to make correct predictions from the story context; that is, whether they could give the correct word even before reading it. They found that the retarded readers were worse at making predictions of this sort. The retarded readers made only 22 per cent correct predictions as against 32 per cent for the normal readers. In other words, the retarded readers relied more heavily on preceding context to aid their word identification even though they were poorer at using context to make predictions. Because their word identification skills were even worse than their prediction skills, it paid them to make as much use of context as possible.

The compensatory hypothesis is important not only because it gives a description of the reading strategies used by retarded readers, but also because it suggests possible ways of improving the reading of these children. It may be possible to help retarded readers by training them to rely more heavily on those components of the reading process in which they are not deficient.

4 Specific reading retardation: The nature of the cognitive deficit

We have seen that retarded readers are frequently found to have major deficiencies in two areas of reading: word identification using phonological recoding; and comprehension of passages where the component words can be adequately identified. In this chapter we will examine some of the evidence which suggests that a basic cognitive deficit may underlie these problems in reading.

One commonly held belief is that specific reading retardation is associated with a deficit in visual perception. This deficit in visual perception supposedly gives rise to confusions between letters like *p, d, b* and *q,* which have the same form but different orientation. It also supposedly causes reversals of sequence such as SPLIT being read as *spilt* and SLAT as *salt*. Certainly, confusions of this sort occur very commonly in *all* children when they are first beginning to read, and there is a tendency for these errors to persist longer in retarded readers. However, it is doubtful that such errors result from a visual perception deficit. When visual perception abilities are tested directly in groups of retarded readers, they are generally found to perform as well as normal readers. For example, I carried out a study in which spatial ability tests were given to groups of retarded readers aged from 8 to 11 years (Jorm, 1977a). One of these tests, called the Pool Reflections Test, required the child to look at an abstract design and pick out the mirror image version of it from a choice of 4 designs. An example of one of the problems on this test is given in Figure 4.1. If retarded readers had some sort of perceptual difficulty which led them to confuse p, b, d and q, then they would certainly have trouble on the Pool Reflections Test. However, retarded readers of all ages were found to do as well as normal readers.

Another example of the evidence against the notion of a visual

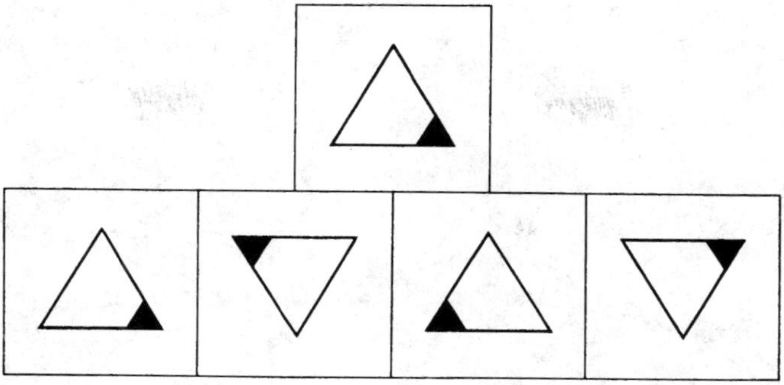

The child has to select the mirror image of the top figure from the four alternatives given below it. (The correct answer is 4.)

Figure 4.1 An item from the Pool Reflections Test

Figure 4.2 Examples of the Hebrew words used by Vellutino and colleagues to test for a visual perception deficit

perception deficit comes from the work of Vellutino and his colleagues (1973). They showed both retarded and normal readers some printed Hebrew words for a brief time. Then immediately afterwards they asked the children to reproduce the printed words from memory. Figure 4.2 shows some of the Hebrew words used in this study. The Hebrew words were completely unfamiliar to the children, so this task provides a test of visual perception and memory for letter-like forms. It was found that the retarded readers performed as well as the normal readers, indicating the visual perception abilities of these children are not impaired.

Given that the cognitive deficit of the retarded readers is not in the area of visual perception, where does it arise? An initial clue as to the nature of this deficit comes from studies of the intelligence test performance of retarded readers. One well-known and commonly used intelligence test is the Wechsler Intelligence Scale for Children, or WISC for short. The WISC consists of 12 subtests, which are grouped into two broad categories, called the Verbal Scale and the Performance Scale. Table 4.1 lists the subtests of the WISC and gives brief descriptions of what each one measures.

The scores on the WISC have been scaled in such a way that, on average, children will get equal scores on the Verbal and Performance Scales. However, there will be individuals who perform much better on one scale than the other, and the pattern of results reveals something about their cognitive strengths and weaknesses. When retarded readers are given the WISC, they tend to perform much worse on the Verbal Scale than on the Performance Scale. As an example, Table 4.2 gives the results of a study by Warrington (1967) which looked at the discrepancy between the Verbal and Performance Scales for a group of retarded readers. It thus appears that the

Table 4.1 The subtests of the Wechsler Intelligence Scale for Children (WISC)

Subtest	*What it involves*
	Verbal scale
Information	Answering factual questions.
Vocabulary	Defining the meanings of words.
Similarities	Pointing to the similarities between two concepts.
Comprehension	Knowing the reasons for social conventions.
Arithmetic	Solving mental arithmetic problems.
Digit span	Holding digits in memory for a short period.
	Performance scale
Block design	Making abstract patterns out of blocks.
Object assembly	Solving jigsaw puzzles.
Picture completion	Finding the missing parts of incomplete pictures.
Picture arrangement	Ordering a series of cartoon pictures to make a story.
Coding	Rapidly writing down the abstract symbols which go with written numbers.
Mazes	Finding the path through a maze printed on paper.

cognitive deficit of retarded readers is to be found in the realm of verbal ability rather than visual perception.

Phonological coding

To gain a more detailed knowledge of this cognitive deficit it is necessary to look to experimental studies which assess specific components of verbal ability. One particular component which seems to be associated with reading difficulties is the ability to deal with phonological information in memory.

Before examining the evidence relating phonological skills and reading ability, it is worth digressing to explain the concept of a *code* in more detail than we have hitherto. This concept was introduced in the last chapter, but it becomes of central importance in this chapter. The concept of a code is best explained by considering the human memory system as being analogous to a tape recorder. Of course, the two are very different, so this analogy should not be taken at all literally. However, there is one very broad similarity. When a tape recorder records speech, it does not hold the actual sounds on the tape. Rather it converts the speech sounds, which are really vibrations in the air, into the form of a magnetic change on the tape. When the tape is played back, these magnetic changes are reconverted to vibrations in the air which are heard as speech sounds. The particular form in which the tape represents the speech sounds could be called a code – an internal representation of the external world. Similarly, the human memory system does not store sound (or any other form of physical energy striking the senses), but uses

Table 4.2 Discrepancies between scores on the Verbal and Performance Scales of the Wechsler Intelligence Scale for Children (WISC)

Difference between Verbal and Performance IQs	% of retarded readers	% of general population
+20 or more	5	6
0 to +19	12	44
-1 to -19	51	44
-20 or more	32	6

Source: Adapted from Warrington (1967).

codes to represent these sources of information in the outer world. Thus, there are visual codes to represent visual information, phonological codes to represent speech information, and semantic codes to represent abstract meaning relationships. A code, then, is a form of internal representation used by the memory system.

Let us now look at the evidence pertaining to the ability of the retarded readers to use phonological codes. Consider what happens when a child is asked to name the object portrayed in a picture as fast as possible. The child presumably converts the picture into a visual code and uses this to find the area in long-term memory where information about the object is stored. Long-term memory contains information about the object's name, stored in a phonological code, which is used to generate a pronunciation. Essentially, this sort of picture naming task requires the child to carry out a recoding operation involving the conversion of a visual code to its phonological equivalent. Several studies have examined the speed with which retarded readers can name pictures, as well as other items such as digits and colours. One of these studies was carried out by Spring and Capps (1974). They tested digit-, picture-, and colour-naming speed in reading retarded and normal boys aged from 7–13 years. Picture-naming speed was tested by having the boys name a block of 25 line drawings of such common objects as a pear, duck, umbrella, and pig. Colour- and digit-naming speeds were tested in a similar fashion. Spring and Capps found that the retarded readers were just as accurate at naming the items as the normal readers, but they were markedly slower. Figure 4.3 shows the results from their study. It can be seen that the differences between the two groups of boys were substantial, with even the *young* normal readers being faster on average than the *old* retarded readers.

The tendency for retarded readers to be slower at retrieving names from long-term memory appears to be present even before they begin learning to read. Biemiller and Bowden (1977) tested the picture naming times of a group of children when they were in Kindergarten. Then two years later, when reading instruction was well underway, they assessed the children's reading performance. They found quite a strong tendency for children who were fast at naming the pictures in Kindergarten to be good readers when subsequently tested in Grade 2.

Not only are retarded readers slow at producing the names of

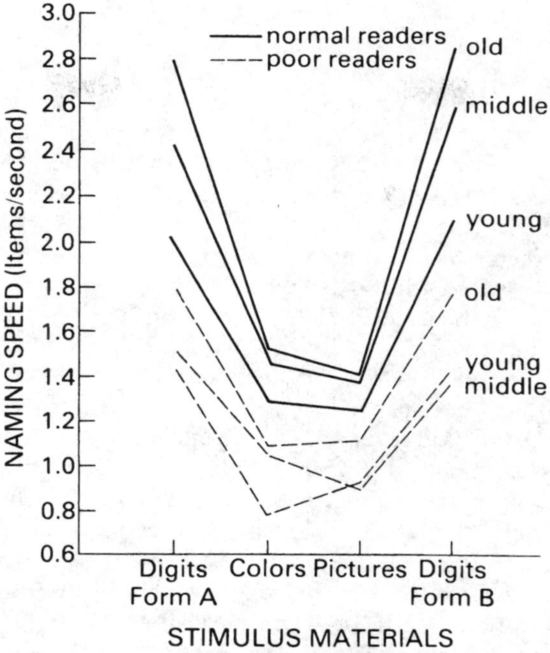

Figure 4.3 Speed of naming colours, digits and pictures
Source: Spring & Capps, 1974

familiar items, but they are also slow to learn the names of unfamiliar items. In other words, they tend to be slow at storing new phonological information in long-term memory. Evidence for this conclusion comes from studies which have attempted to teach retarded readers to give nonsense word names in response to unfamiliar line drawings. Several such studies have been carried out by Vellutino and his colleagues. In one of these studies (Vellutino, Steger, Harding and Phillips, 1975), retarded and normal readers were required to associate spoken nonsense words with either nonsense animal shapes or with word-like squiggles. The materials that the children had to learn are shown in Figure 4.4. To test a child's learning of the nonsense names, the researchers would show the child a nonsense animal or a squiggle and ask for its name. If the child could not give the correct name, the researcher would supply the answer and then go on to the next nonsense animal or squiggle. This sort of testing procedure went on until the child learned all the names, or otherwise it was stopped when he or she had been tested a total of 10 times for each name. The retarded readers were found to be much slower to learn the nonsense names than the normal readers. The retarded readers who learned names for the nonsense animals scored an average of 13 out of 40 correct, as against 22 out of 40 for the normal readers. Similarly, in learning names for the word-like squiggles, the retarded readers scored only 16 out of 40 compared to 25 out of 40 for the normal readers.

Despite their difficulties in learning to associate names with objects, retarded readers appear to have no problems in memory for meaning. In other words, their semantic coding ability tends to be normal. In fact, when retarded readers are asked to learn nonsense word names for unfamiliar items, they seem to try to process these names semantically rather than phonologically. In Vellutino's study, for instance, the retarded readers tended to make different sorts of errors when they misnamed a figure, compared to the normal readers. When the normal readers made errors, they tended to give another nonsense word which sounded similar to the correct name, e.g., WIB might be recalled as WUB. The retarded readers, on the other hand, had a much greater tendency to respond with a real word when they made an error, e.g., WIB might be recalled as WHIP. This finding suggests that the retarded readers may have been trying to impose meaning on the nonsense words in the attempt to remember them.

There is other more direct evidence that retarded readers perform as well as normal readers in memory tasks which require semantic coding. In the previous chapter we saw that retarded readers perform quite adequately when required to associate *real words* with word-like squiggles. It is only when retarded readers are confronted with tasks requiring the storage or rapid retrieval of phonological information that difficulties arise.

So far we have considered phonological coding ability in terms of simple naming tasks. However, phonological coding comes into play whenever we have to remember the exact wording of what we hear or read. An example of this is in learning a poem by heart or the lines for a role in a play. In these situations, it is not sufficient to recall the meaning – the exact wording of the original must be recalled as well. In fact, there is evidence that retarded readers have difficulty with tasks which require memory for wording as well as memory for meaning. A study by Waller (1976) provides some neat evidence in support of this conclusion. Waller tested fifth grade

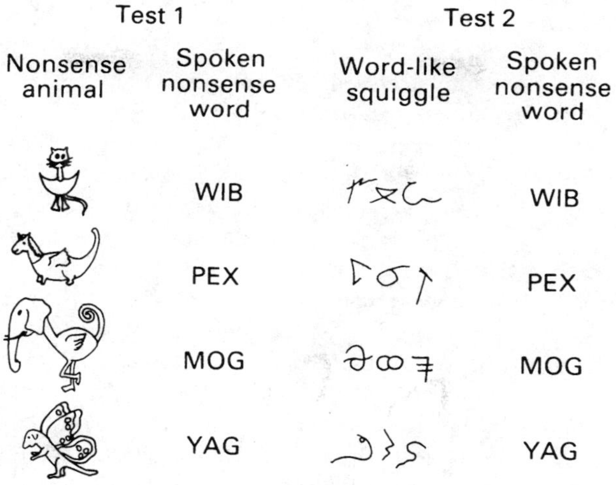

Test 1
Test 2
Nonsense animal
Spoken nonsense word
Word-like squiggle
Spoken nonsense word
WIB
WIB
PEX
PEX
MOG
MOG
YAG
YAG

Figure 4.4 Materials used to test the ability of retarded readers to associate spoken nonsense words with visual shapes

Source: Adapted from Vellutino, Steger, Harding and Phillips, 1975.

retarded and normal readers on their memory for some simple 'stories' he gave them to read. These so-called stories were not stories in the true sense, but series of short sentences about a topic. An example of one of Waller's stories is:

The bird is inside the cage.
The cage is under the table.
The bird is yellow.

After reading eight stories similar to this, the children were shown some sentences and had to say whether or not each sentence had appeared in a story. Basically, this was a yes/no test of memory for the sentences which made up the stories. Some of the test sentences were identical with those appearing earlier in the stories, e.g., *The bird is inside the cage.* With sentences such as these, the retarded readers did as well as the normal readers. However, other test sentences had not appeared in the stories. Some of these sentences had a different meaning from that conveyed in the original story, e.g., *The bird is over the table,* while others retained the meaning of the original, but had not actually appeared in a story, e.g., *The bird is under the table.* Consider what a child would need to have stored in memory to respond *no* to such sentences. In the first case (*The bird is over the table*), where the meaning of the test sentence differs from the original story, the child would only need to have stored a representation of the story's meaning in memory to realise that it could not have been in the story. In the second case, however (*The bird is under the table*), where the meaning of the test sentence is true, the child needs to have stored information about the wording of the original story as well as its meaning. To be specific, the child has to remember that the story said the *cage* is under the table, even though this in effect implies that the bird is under the table as well. Waller found that the retarded readers were as good as the normal readers at saying *no* to sentences like *The bird is over the table,* but were worse with sentences like *The bird is under the table,* which required memory for specific wording.

Working Memory

So far we have dealt with what might be called long-term memory for phonological information. That is, we have seen that retarded readers are deficient in tasks which require them to retrieve phonological codes stored permanently in memory (e.g., picture names), or to establish and hold new phonological codes for more than a few minutes. However, the human memory system also has the capability of holding small amounts of phonological information for relatively brief periods without necessarily committing it to long-term memory.

A classic example of this form of short-term memory involves looking up an unfamiliar number in the telephone book. We are able to hold this information in memory long enough for us to dial the number, but afterwards it is promptly forgotten. One noteworthy feature of this short-term memory is its quite limited capacity. For instance, if we are looking up a telephone number which contains 6 digits we will probably have little trouble retaining it long enough to dial, but if the number had 15 digits the task would become extremely difficult. Although the capacity of short-term memory is limited, it is not fixed in any simple way. How much information we can hold in short-term memory depends crucially on our familiarity with the type of material we are trying to remember. For example, although most people have great difficulty trying to hold a telephone number of more than 7 digits in short-term memory, people who are very well practiced at this task can do far better because of their great familiarity with number sequences.

One might wonder what is the point of having a memory storage system which allows us to retain telephone numbers for a brief period. However, it seems that brief storage of small amounts of information is necessary to allow us to carry out everyday cognitive tasks. Take, for example, mental arithmetic. Try adding up the following series of numbers and introspect on your mental processes while you are doing it:

$$9 + 13 + 6 + 20 + 5 + 7 = ?$$

What you may have done was to take the first number, 9, and add 13 to it to get a subtotal of 22. Next, you may have added 6 to this subtotal, giving a new subtotal of 28, and so on. At each step of this process, a subtotal was generated and the next number was added to this. However, once a new subtotal is produced, the old one is forgotten. A subtotal is retained in short-term memory just as long as it is useful, and then it is discarded. Imagine that there was no short-term memory to hold the subtotals and that they had to be stored in long-term memory. Long-term memory would then get cluttered up with a lot of useless information. For this reason, it is important that certain types of information be stored in a non-permanent form.

Although mental arithmetic was chosen as a specific example, many other cognitive tasks require the use of a temporary storage system. Some psychologists use the term *working memory* to refer to this temporary storage system in order to emphasise the important role it plays in the execution of so many everyday cognitive tasks. In fact, working memory is probably not a single memory store, but a series of interrelated memory stores, each specialising in the retention of specific types of information. One of these working memory stores, referred to by Baddeley and Hitch (1974) as the *articulatory loop,* appears to be specialised at holding phonological information. It is called the *articulatory* loop because it is believed to hold speech information in a form closely related to its articulation or production. During the execution of complex tasks requiring the brief retention of phonological information, this articulatory loop is supplied with phonological codes stored permanently in long-term memory. However, if phonological codes are not available in long-term memory, or cannot be accessed rapidly enough, then the articulatory loop cannot play its role. In fact, there is now a reasonable amount of evidence that retarded readers have difficulty in utilising the articulatory loop adequately and this may reflect problems in accessing phonological codes in long-term memory. Let us look at some of the studies supporting this conclusion.

If retarded readers have a problem in utilising the articulatory loop, then we might expect them to be poor at holding a series of digits in short-term memory. In fact, when retarded readers are given the WISC, they are frequently found to do poorly on the Digit Span subtest. In the Digit Span subtest, children are given a series of digits at the rate of one digit every second. In one part of the subtest, they have to repeat the digits back in the same order, while in the other part the children have to give the reverse order. The length of the digit strings is gradually increased until the child can no longer repeat them correctly. However, a small digit span is not found in all retarded readers. A study by Torgesen and Houck (1980) tried to find out the reasons for the digit span deficit which occurs in some retarded readers. They divided retarded readers into two groups, those with a digit span deficit and those without, and compared their performance on various memory tasks to a group of normal readers. One of their most interesting findings was that there is a relationship between a child's digit span and the speed with which that child can name digits presented visually. Children who were fast at naming digits also tended to have larger digit spans, suggesting that speed of accessing phonological codes in long-term memory is an important factor in determining digit span. Consider what happens when a child hears 6 digits spoken at a rate of 1 every second and must retain these in working memory. The child must be able to generate an internal code for each digit that is presented and must hold this code in a suitable store such as the articulatory loop. However, if the code for a particular digit cannot be retrieved before the next digit is presented, the child will be unable to retain all the digits adequately. The child must either abandon the search for the code of the previous digit, or else continue the search and ignore the incoming digit. In this way, coding speed can reduce the effective working memory capacity.

Because the articulatory loop holds information in a phonological code, it is prone to errors which involve confusions of similar-sounding items. For example, if somebody attempts to hold a number-plate like PTB 592 in working memory, they may erroneously recall it as PTD 592, because B and D are so similar in sound. Another way of looking at such phonological confusions is to compare people's memory for series of letters or words which are very similar in sound (e.g., B, T, D, P, G, C, or MAD, GLAD, SAD, DAD, PAD) with memory for series of dissimilar-sounding items (e.g., B, K, X, Y, Q, R, or CAT, FOX, HOLD, RED, SKY). It is generally found that the similar-sounding series of items are harder to recall accurately than the dissimilar-sounding series. This finding applies even if the items are presented visually, indicating that when people have to commit printed material to short-term memory, they tend to convert it to a phonological code even though it was not originally presented in spoken form. If retarded readers have difficulty in utilising the articulatory loop, then we might expect them to be *less* prone to phonological confusions of this sort. In fact, several studies with young retarded readers have found this to be the case. For example, Shankweiler and his colleagues (1979) tested superior, marginal and poor Second Grade readers on short-term memory for series of letters which were either rhyming or non-rhyming; for example, B C D G P and H K L Q R. These series of letters were presented by several different methods: they were either spoken one letter at a time, shown on a screen one letter at a time, or all letters were shown on a screen simultaneously. However, whatever the method of presenting the letters, the results were the same. The poor readers showed poorer recall overall, but were less affected by the rhyming letters than were the marginal and good readers. The results of this experiment are shown in Figure 4.5. It can be seen from this graph that the superior readers showed a marked difference between their ability to recall the rhyming letters and their ability to recall the non-rhyming ones.

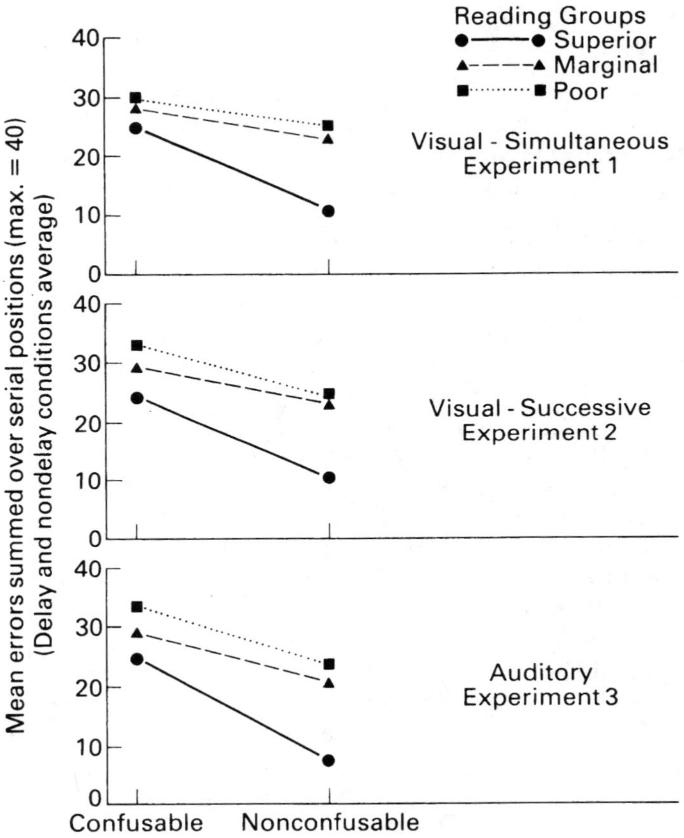

Figure 4.5 Ability to remember rhyming and non-rhyming letters

Source: Shankweiler *et al.*, 1979.

However, for the poor and marginal readers there was less difference between the amounts which could be recalled for the two types of items.

This sort of finding is not confined to memory for letter series. It has been found with sentences as well. Mann, Liberman and Shankweiler (1980), for example, compared short-term recall of phonologically confusable sentences with that of non-confusable ones. Here are some examples of the two types of sentence:

> Confusable: Jack and Mack stacked sacks on the track in back of the shack.
> Non-confusable: Tom and Bill piled books on the chair in front of the door.

Even with meaningful sentences like these, the same sort of results were found. The good readers found the confusable sentences far harder to recall than the non-confusable ones, but for the retarded readers there was little difference in recall between the two types of sentences. Nevertheless, the good readers were better over all at recalling the sentences than were the retarded readers. It seems then that good readers may perform better on short-term recall tasks because they are able to use the articulatory loop to hold the information in a phonological code. However, it can sometimes be disadvantageous to use the articulatory loop, as when the material that has to be retained is phonologically confusable. In these circumstances, the short-term recall of good readers is little better than that of retarded readers.

Another feature of the articulatory loop is that it holds information about the *order* in which items are presented. To illustrate this point, let us hark back to our earlier example of storing an unfamiliar telephone number for a brief period. In order to dial the correct number, it is not sufficient to dial the digits in any order; we have to remember the exact order of the digits as well. The articulatory loop seems to be specialised for holding order information of this type. Since the articulatory loop plays such an important role in retaining order information in working memory, we might expect retarded readers to have particular difficulty in retaining the order of items. A study by Mason, Katz and Wicklund (1975) attempted to assess retarded readers' short-term memory for order information. In one of their experiments, children who were either retarded or normal readers were shown lists of 8 letters for a few seconds each. During this time, the children had to read each letter aloud. Immediately after a list of letters had been presented, the children had to recall them. Mason, Katz and Wicklund used two different methods of assessing how much the children recalled. One method was to ask the children to write down as many letters as they could *in any order*.

This method tested the children's memory for the letters, but not memory for their order. The second method was to give the children the letters on some small tiles and have them place these letters in the correct order. In this method, the children had to remember the order of the letters, but not which particular letters were presented. Mason, Katz and Wicklund found that the good readers were better than the retarded readers at remembering both the letters and their order. However, memory for order appeared to have a greater relationship to reader ability than did memory for the items. The results of this study seem to be consistent with the idea of an articulatory loop deficit which affects the ability to retain order information.

To summarise the argument so far: reading retardation appears to be often associated with a deficiency in the storage and retrieval of phonological codes in long-term memory. This long-term phonological memory deficit may affect the functioning of working memory, specifically the articulatory loop which is specialised for the temporary storage of a small amount of phonologically coded information. Let us now examine how a memory deficit of this sort might affect reading performance.

Working memory deficit and reading ability

In the previous chapter we saw that readers can access the meaning of a word stored in long-term memory by either of two mechanisms: they can find the meaning directly on the basis of a visual analysis of the printed word, or they can convert the printed word into a phonological code using letter-to-sound conversion. Furthermore, we saw that there is evidence that retarded readers have grave difficulties in reading via the phonological recoding mechanism. The obvious question to ask is whether a deficit in working memory could affect this mechanism. In fact, it seems quite likely that working memory plays an important role in word identification via phonological recoding. Let us consider what might be happening when a child has to work out an unfamiliar word or a nonsense word. As a specific example, we will look at the sort of process that might go on in generating a pronunciation for the nonsense word SANPLIN. First of all, the child converts the S into its sound. This sound must be stored somewhere while the child is working on the following letters. A likely place for storing the sound is the articulatory loop. Next the child converts the A to its sound and this is also stored in the articulatory loop. Note that the child has to remember not only both sounds but also the order in which they occurred. The child then converts the N to its sound and can now blend the three sounds *s-a-n* into the single syllable *san*. Now, instead of holding three sounds in the articulatory loop, the child has only to hold one syllable. The child works through the letters, P, L, I and N in the same way: converting each in turn to its sound and holding this in the articulatory loop while the other letters are being worked on. Finally, the child can blend the four sounds into the single syllable *plin* which is stored in the articulatory loop. When the two syllables *san* and *plin* are finally blended together, the child has generated a pronunciation for the nonsense word. It is easy to see that the storage of phonological information in working memory might play a very important role in the reading of words by letter-to-sound conversion.

The second area of reading where retarded readers have difficulties is in comprehension. In the previous chapter, we saw that these children do not comprehend as well as might be expected even when they can identify the individual words in a passage. Again, a working memory deficiency could be partly responsible for this comprehension problem. Working memory may play an important role in several aspects of reading comprehension. The reason working memory may be necessary is that when sentences are read only one or two words can be processed at a time, but the meaning of the whole sentence can only be derived by relating the early words in the sentence to the later words. This is a rather abstract point which is best explained by reference to some concrete examples. We will look at three specific examples of where working memory appears to play a crucial role in reading comprehension.

As a first example, try reading each of the following sentences, taking note of how easy or difficult each is to comprehend.

1 The sun shone on the hot desert sands.
2 The moon which was low on the horizon provided a delicate light on the ocean.
3 The wind which blew from the tall mountain range situated in the south-east of the country cooled the hot corrugated iron roof.

What you probably found was that Sentence 1 was relatively easy to comprehend, Sentence 2 slightly harder, and Sentence 3 hardest of all. In fact, you may have had to reread portions of Sentence 3 in order to work out its meaning. The obvious difference between the three sentences is their length. However, there are other differences which may be of greater significance as far as ease of comprehension goes. Notice the number of words separating the subject of each sentence and the verb that goes with it. In Sentence 1, the subject and its verb are adjacent:

> The *sun shone* on the hot desert sands.

However, in Sentences 2 and 3 the verb is separated from its subject by another clause.

> The *moon* which was low on the horizon *provided* a delicate light on the ocean.
> The *wind* which blew from the tall mountain range situated in the south-east of the country *cooled* the corrugated iron roof.

In each of these cases, the reader has to hold the subject of the sentence in working memory until the verb is processed, otherwise the sentence could not be understood. For example, a child who reads Sentence 3 and forgets *wind* before coming to *cooled* will have to reread the sentence in order to comprehend it.

A second example of the role of working memory in reading comprehension is in the understanding of pronouns like *I, she, it, they,* etc. Take the following sentence which contains a number of pronouns.

> There was once a farmer who had a clever sheep-dog which he loved very much.

When the pronoun *he* is encountered we must relate it to the noun to which it refers, namely *farmer*. Similarly, the *who* must be related to *farmer* and the *which* to *sheep-dog*. These nouns must be stored in working memory if the reader is to work out what each of the pronouns refers to. If the reader does not have the appropriate referent for a pronoun stored in working memory, then the earlier part of the sentence may have to be reread to supply it.

A third area where working memory may be important is in the comprehension of sentences where word order is important. Remember that the articulatory loop component of working memory is specialised in holding order information. The importance of word order in reading comprehension can be seen in a sentence such as:

> Sydney is bigger than Adelaide which is smaller than Melbourne.

For the reader unfamiliar with Australian cities, correct processing of the exact positions of *Sydney, Melbourne* and *Adelaide* in the sentence is of great importance to its correct interpretation. In fact, this sentence will have to be reread if word order information is not properly retained in working memory. Another sentence in which word order appears to be particularly crucial is the following:

> Push the red button with your right index finger and then pull the blue lever hard with your left hand.

Anyone reading this instruction in a manual could easily end up trying to push a red lever with their left hand if they did not process word order satisfactorily.

Having seen that a phonological coding deficit can lead to great difficulties in reading, it seems appropriate to ask what causes this deficit. In the next chapter, we will examine evidence that such a deficit may, in part, come about from factors in brain development.

5 Specific reading retardation: Brain development

It is likely that there are a whole host of factors contributing to specific reading retardation, including such environmental factors as inadequate teaching and lack of stimulation at home. However, biological factors, such as individual differences in brain development, also seem to contribute. In fact, when people use the term *dyslexic* to refer to children with specific reading difficulties, the usual implication is that some biological deficit underlies the problem. In this section, we will examine some of the evidence for the role of biological factors.

A number of studies have been carried out to examine the role of genetic factors in reading difficulties. A piece of evidence often cited in support of this notion is that reading difficulties tend to run in families. For example, a study by Finucci, Guthrie, Childs, Abbey and Childs (1976) looked at the incidence of reading problems in the families of 20 children who were retarded readers. In 16 families they were able to test the reading performance of both the child's parents. The results they found were as follows:

Children with both parents retarded readers	3
Children with one parent a retarded reader	10
Children with no parent a retarded reader	3
Total no. of families 16	

Altogether, this study examined the reading performance of 75 members of the immediate families of the 20 retarded readers: parents, brothers, and sisters. In 45 per cent of the cases these immediate family members were also retarded readers, showing the quite strong tendency for reading retardation to run in families. Although findings such as these are consistent with the idea that reading retardation is in part associated with genetic factors, it is equally possible that reading problems run in families for environmental reasons. For example, if a child's parents cannot read well themselves they may provide a less stimulating home environment where books are scarce and the children are seldom read to or encouraged to read themselves. Finucci and colleagues counter this argument by pointing out that in all the families they studied, the parents were greatly concerned about their child's reading retardation and had sought specialised remedial help for the problem. They also note that the retarded readers often had brothers and sisters who were very good readers despite growing up in the same family environment. Although arguments such as these sound convincing, we can never be completely certain from studies such as this what the reason is for reading retardation running in families.

To discover whether genetic factors play a role we need a different sort of evidence, and researchers have turned to the well-known method of studying the similarities of twins. Most people will know that twins are of two varieties: identical twins who share exactly the same genetic make-up, and fraternal twins who are only as genetically similar as any other pair of children from the same family. To be more specific, identical twins share 100 per cent of their genes in common, while fraternal twins share approximately 50 per cent. Because identical twins are exactly alike genetically, any differences which are observed between them must be due to differences in their environments. For example, if identical twin A is found to be an outstanding reader while his twin brother B is only average, then this difference must have arisen because of some environmental advantage for twin A (e.g., superior instruction). With fraternal twins, on the other hand, any differences between them could be due to either environmental or genetic factors, since they differ in both respects. Assuming that both identical and fraternal twins have equally similar environments, we have a basis for assessing the role of genetic factors in producing individual differences.*

If fraternal twins are found to be less alike in some characteristic than identical twins, then it is likely that genetic factors contribute somewhat to individual differences.

Some studies of this sort were carried out with retarded readers during the 1950s by Scandinavian researchers. These researchers

*It is perhaps worth noting that the assumption of equally similar environments for identical and fraternal twins has been questioned by Coles (1980). He argues that identical twins are in fact treated more alike than are fraternal twins. If Coles is correct, twin studies would not provide a good basis for studying the role of genetic factors in reading retardation.

located children with severe reading retardation who were also twins and then saw whether the other twin of the pair was also retarded at reading. The results of these studies were summarised by Hermann (1959). With 12 sets of identical twins, it was found that in all cases both twins had reading difficulties. However, with 33 sets of fraternal twins, it was found that in only 11 cases did both twins have reading difficulties. In the other 22 cases, one twin had reading difficulties but the other twin did not. These results clearly indicate a role for genetic factors in reading retardation.

Other studies have looked at the relative similarities of identical and fraternal twins over the whole range of reading ability. These studies assess the similarity of twins in reading ability by the use of correlation coefficients. The technical details of correlation coefficients need not concern us here. It is enough to know that a correlation coefficient of 1 indicates that each twin is exactly like his or her partner in reading ability, and a correlation of 0 indicates that there is no systematic relationship between the members of a pair in their reading ability. Correlation coefficients generally lie in between 0 and 1, with higher coefficients indicating greater similarity between pairs of twins. The results of three studies of this sort are summarised in Table 5.1.

As you can see, in all three studies the fraternal twins were found to be less alike in reading ability than the identical twins, indicating a role of genetic factors in producing individual differences in reading ability.

Although genetic factors seem to play some role in reading

Table 5.1

Author(s) of study	*How reading was assessed*	*Correlation coefficient* *Identical Twins*	*Fraternal Twins*
Matheny and Dolan (1974)	California Achievement Test	.89	.61
Husen (1960)	Reading Achievement Tests	.89	.62
Newman, Freeman and Holzinger (1937)	Stanford Achievement Test: Word Meaning	.86	.56

retardation, this should not be interpreted to mean that reading problems are somehow innate or fixed. Unfortunately, the results of twin studies are often erroneously interpreted to mean just that. However, reading is definitely a skill acquired through teaching and it is a skill that can be improved in any child through more or better teaching.

Twin studies tell us something about why children end up differing in their reading achievement – specifically what contribution genetic or environmental factors make to these differences, but they say nothing about whether or not reading difficulties can be remediated. To make this issue clearer, imagine two boys, John and Tasman, who are given *exactly* the same reading instruction. However, John turns out to be an average reader while Tasman is well below average. How can this difference be explained? It is possible that John has had some environmental advantage over Tasman which has produced the difference, but another alternative is that John was genetically predisposed to profit more from reading instruction than Tasman. Imagine, for argument's sake, that the second alternative is correct and John has a genetic advantage over Tasman. Now if both boys had been given some superior form of reading instruction they might both have achieved far better, with John becoming an above average reader and Tasman an average reader. Although both boys would be now considerably better at reading because of the superior instruction, they still differ in achievement because John is genetically predisposed to profit more from the instruction. Now let's take this argument a step further. Just say we had given John the ordinary instruction and Tasman the superior instruction. In this case, both boys might have ended up being average readers despite John's genetic advantage over Tasman. It should be clear from this imaginary example that, although genetic factors may produce differences between people in reading achievement, they do not necessarily limit a person's potential for becoming a skilled reader under suitable circumstances.

Given that genetic factors can give rise to differences between children in reading achievement, they must affect reading acquisition indirectly through some effect on brain function. In fact, there is evidence showing that retarded readers sometimes differ from normal readers in certain aspects of brain function. However, before looking at some of this evidence, it is necessary to know a few basic facts about the brain.

Organisation of the brain

The most notable feature of the brain is that it is divided into two halves called the *cerebral hemispheres*. Although the brains of other mammals also have two hemispheres, the human brain is unique in that the two hemispheres are very different in the sort of psychological functions they serve. The left hemisphere of the brain is generally specialised for language functions, so that if a person gets damage to this half of the brain he or she may have difficulty with such tasks as speaking, comprehending speech, reading, and spelling. The right hemisphere, on the other hand, tends to be specialised for non-language abilities like orientation in space and perception of music. People who have damage to this half of the brain may show disorders in such abilities as recognising faces, reading maps, and appreciation of music. Although this pattern of hemispheric specialisation is true of most people, there is a small minority who show the reversed pattern, with right hemisphere specialisation for language abilities and left hemisphere specialisation for non-language abilities.

Since the left hemisphere tends to be specialised for language abilities, we would expect that if reading retardation involves a deficit of brain function, it would be the left hemisphere which is deficient rather than the right one. In fact, there is some recent and quite exciting research which indicates that specific reading retardation may sometimes be associated with a deficiency of the left hemisphere. A fascinating study by some medical researchers, Hier, Le May, Rosenberger and Perlo (1978), examined the brains of retarded readers directly using the newly developed technique of *computerised brain tomography*. This technique allows the brain itself to be seen by X-ray. Previous X-ray techniques could detect bones but not soft body tissues like the brain. Researchers who have taken computerised tomograms of normal adult brains have found that the two hemispheres of the brain are not generally equal in size. In most people, the back part of the left hemisphere is found to be slightly larger than the back part of the right hemisphere. This difference has even been found in the brains of infants. In other words, the hemisphere dealing with language is generally found to be bigger than the non-language hemisphere. An example of a computerised tomogram showing this typical pattern is shown in Figure 5.1a. However, Hier and his colleagues found that in adults with specific reading retardation there is a high incidence of the reversed pattern, with the right hemisphere being bigger than the

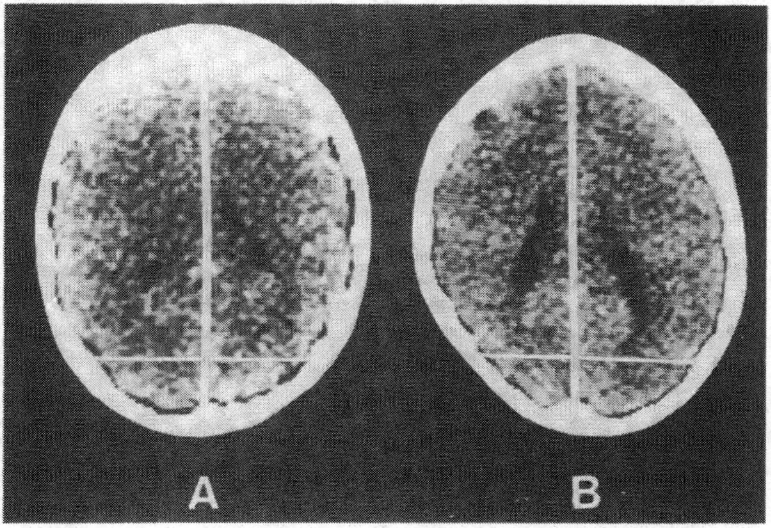

Fig. 5.1 Computerised tomograms of human brains
Brain (a) shows a larger left hemisphere while brain (b) shows a larger right hemisphere

Source: Hier *et al.*, 1978

left hemisphere. That is, the hemisphere dealing with language tends to be smaller in retarded readers. An example of this reversed pattern appears in Figure 5.1b. Altogether, Hier and his colleagues obtained tomograms of the brains of 24 adults who were retarded readers. They found that 10 had brains that were wider on the right; 8 had brains that were wider on the left; and 6 had brains that were roughly equal in both hemispheres. On the basis of previous research using normal adults, it would be expected that only about 3 out of a group of 24 adults would show the reversed pattern of a wider right hemisphere. It therefore appears that retarded readers have a much greater tendency to have a smaller language hemisphere, although this pattern is by no means true of all retarded readers. Hier and his colleagues also tested these retarded readers on the Wechsler Adult Intelligence Scale – an adult version of the Wechsler Intelligence Scale for Children which was described earlier. They were particularly interested in comparing the Verbal IQs with the Performance

IQs in these retarded readers. You may recall that research on children with specific reading retardation has shown that they generally are lower in Verbal IQ than in Performance IQ. However, Hier and colleagues found this pattern to be more marked in the retarded readers with right hemispheres wider than their left. These individuals had an average Verbal IQ of 87 and an average Performance IQ of 96 – a discrepancy of 9 points. However, the individuals who had wider left hemispheres or equal-sized hemispheres were found to have an average Verbal IQ of 99 and an average Performance IQ of 103 – a discrepancy of only 4 points. In other words, if a person's left hemisphere is relatively smaller, they tend to be poorer on verbal tasks generally, as might be expected given that the left hemisphere plays a dominant role in language skills for most people.

There is other evidence indicating that left hemisphere deficiencies may have a role in specific reading retardation. Several studies have looked at the electrical activity of the brain in retarded readers. By attaching small electrodes to the scalp it is possible to record the electrical activity of the brain which passes through the skull. The electrical changes involved are very small and require a special sensitive machine called an *electroencephalogram* for their measurement. These electrical changes are often drawn as waves on moving graph paper as shown in Figure 5.2. The resulting graph of the 'brain waves' is known as the *electroencephalograph,* or *EEG* for short. Naturally, only a small part of the complex electrical activity of the brain can be recorded from the scalp, so visual inspection of the EEG tends to be a rather crude measure which can accurately reflect only such gross psychological states as alertness, drowsiness, deep sleep, and dreaming. Visual inspection of the EEG can sometimes also be used to detect damage to the brain, as when there is a tumour, but unfortunately it cannot detect such brain damage with great reliability. Although many studies have looked for differences between the EEGs of normal and retarded readers, the results are not clear-cut because of the crude nature of the measurement involved. However, one EEG study by Hanley and Sklar (1976) is exceptional in this regard. Rather than simply carry out a visual inspection for obvious abnormalities in the EEG, they did a complex computer analysis of the EEG waves of retarded and normal readers and found a number of differences between the two

Figure 5.2 An EEG record

Source: Einon, Geoff S. (ed.), *Introduction to the Nervous System*, Open University Press, Milton Keynes, 1974, p. 17.

groups. The important aspect of their results is not the nature of the electrical differences they found, but in the areas of the scalp where these differences were recorded. The major difference between the EEG patterns of the retarded and normal readers was in the recordings taken from the scalp above the back part of the left hemisphere. This result is quite consistent with the findings from computerised tomography and indicates a possible deficit in the functioning of the hemisphere specialised for language.

A slightly more refined measure of the electrical activity of the brain is the *evoked potential.* The evoked potential is measured using the same sort of equipment as the EEG. However, rather than measuring the ongoing activity of the brain, the evoked potential measures the electrical response to a stimulus such as a flash of light or a printed word presented for a brief time. When such a stimulus is presented it leads to a change in the EEG which lasts for less than a second. It is this brief change which is the evoked potential. In actual practice, the evoked potential cannot be measured accurately after only one stimulus because there is so much electrical interference from other processes going on in the brain at the same time. What researchers must do is present the same stimulus and record the resulting evoked potential over and over again and then average the results to remove the effects of interference. Several groups of researchers have compared the evoked potentials of normal and retarded readers and have found some reasonably consistent and interesting differences. The first study of this type was published by Conners in 1970. He studied the evoked potential to a flash of light from a family of retarded readers. In this family there was an 11 year old boy who had severe reading difficulties. This boy was reading at a level worse than an average second grade child. As is often found, other members of the boy's family also had reading difficulties. His brother, two sisters, and father were also retarded readers, although the mother was a normal reader. Furthermore, the boy's uncle on his father's side and his paternal grandmother were retarded readers, while his paternal grandfather and all his relatives on his mother's side appeared to be normal readers. Conners recorded the visual evoked potentials in each of these family members from four different locations on the scalp – two on the left side of the head and two on the right side. The electrodes placed over the left side of the head are the ones of most interest, because these were above the hemisphere specialised for language functions like reading. One of these electrodes was placed above the left parietal region of the brain which appears to be important in language skills, particularly reading, whereas the other electrode was above the left occipital region which is specialised for the processing of visual information. Figure 5.3 shows a diagram of the brain as seen from the left side, with the parietal and occipital regions marked. Conners found that the boy with specific reading retardation showed an unusual flattening of the evoked potential waveform recorded from above the left parietal region compared to the evoked potentials from the other electrodes.

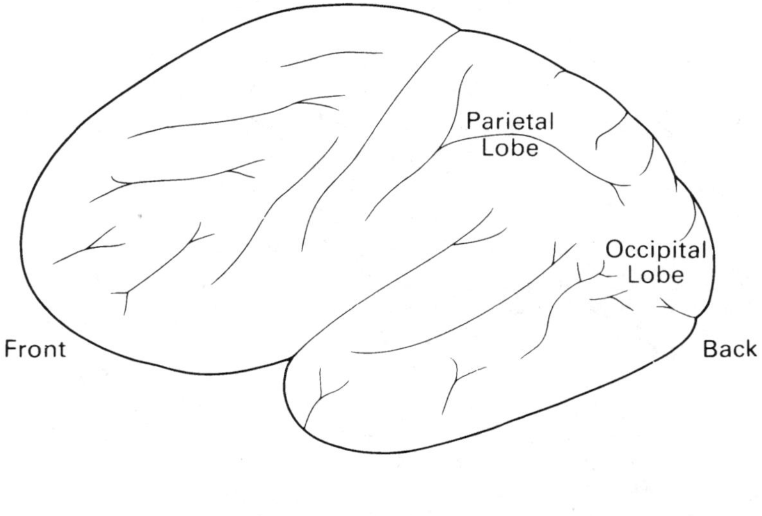

Figure 5.3 Human brain looked at from the left side

This flattening can be clearly seen in the evoked potential wave shown in Figure 5.4. Many other members of the boy's family showed a similar flattening of the evoked potential from this region. Conners later followed up this finding by recording visual evoked potentials from groups of children with reading retardation. He found similar results in many of these children: an unusual response from the left parietal region, but not from the left occipital region or from the right hemisphere.

Other groups of researchers have continued on from where Conners left off and have tried to extend and refine his findings. Although some researchers have been unable to find the same flattening of the visual evoked potential recorded from above the left parietal region, others have found similar results. Later researchers have made the sensible step of looking at evoked potentials in response to written words rather than flashes of light. If some retarded readers do have a deficiency in the functioning of the left hemisphere, then we would

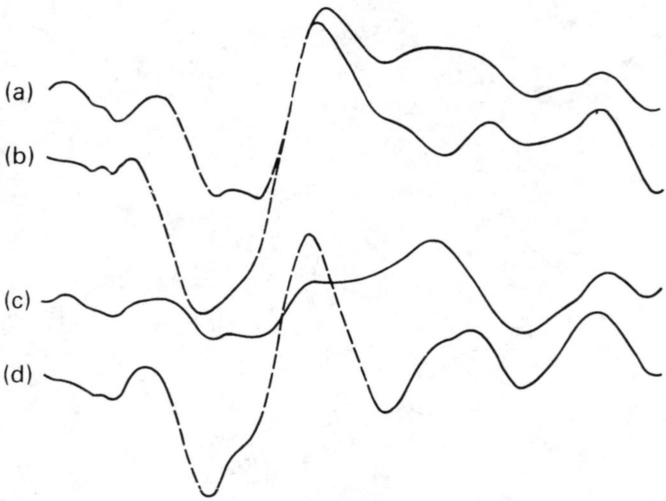

Figure 5.4 Evoked potentials from the (a) left occipital (b) right occipital (c) left parietal and (d) right parietal regions of a retarded reader

Source: Conners, 1970.

expect it to show particularly during the act of reading. A number of studies using this technique (Symann-Lovett, Gascon, Matsumiya and Lombroso, 1977; Preston, Guthrie and Childs, 1974) have shown that the evoked potentials of retarded readers are flatter when recorded from above the left parietal region. This finding has even been extended to the *parents* of children who are retarded readers (Preston, Guthrie, Kirsch, Gertman and Childs, 1977).

In conclusion, both research using computerised tomography and research using evoked potentials indicates that reading retardation can be associated with deficient functioning of the left hemisphere. This finding is quite consistent with our earlier conclusion that difficulties in language skills – in particular the storage and retrieval of phonological information in long-term memory – are important in producing reading retardation.

6 Reading comprehension disabilities

Specific reading retardation has excited a lot of research interest. The preceding chapters have reviewed only a small amount of this research. The literature on the topic is so vast that it would be impossible to be other than selective in reviewing it. Other types of reading disability, on the other hand, have been largely ignored by researchers. One group of problems which have received little attention are the reading comprehension disabilities. Children with this type of disability can identify individual words quite adequately, but still have difficulties with text comprehension. In fact, some people have suggested that reading problems of this type may not even exist (Calfee, Arnold and Drum, 1976). They point out that there is a very strong relationship between the ability to read individual words and the ability to comprehend text: children who are good at identifying individual words are very likely to be good at text comprehension as well, and children who are poor at word identification are very likely to be poor at comprehending text. However, although there is a strong relationship between these two abilities, it is not a perfect one and discrepancies do exist. There is a very small minority of children whose comprehension of text lags significantly behind their ability to identify the individual words in the text.

Perhaps the major reason that reading comprehension disabilities have been ignored is that so little is known about how we extract the meaning of what we read. It is only in the last few years that we have even begun to get some conception of the cognitive processes involved. Of course, without understanding reading comprehension as it occurs in skilled readers we cannot understand comprehension disabilities in unskilled readers.

Because of the dearth of research on the topic, this chapter is rather different in character from any other in the book. Rather than examining what has already been discovered about reading comprehension disabilities, it often speculates on what might be discovered in the future. These speculations are based on the understanding we are beginning to have about the process of comprehension in the skilled reader.

The experience of specific comprehension problems

Most people have occasionally experienced what it feels like to have a specific comprehension problem. One instance of this phenomenon is in reading highly technical material, such as an advanced science textbook. With this sort of material it is often possible to read all the individual words correctly and yet not understand the author's point. The problem in this case is usually that the reader lacks the relevant background knowledge which is necessary for understanding the ideas being presented. However, if the reader were first to take a course of study in the particular subject area, in order to gain the necessary background knowledge, he or she would possibly then be able to comprehend the text.

Another instance of this sort of experience sometimes occurs to people when they learn a foreign language. Some European languages have a very regular relationship between print and sound. With a knowledge of the print-to-sound relationships of these languages it is possible to read aloud with reasonable fluency and yet not be able to comprehend what is being read. In this case, poor comprehension results because of an imperfect knowledge of the language in question and not because of any problem in understanding the content itself. After further study of the language, comprehension would become possible.

From these two examples it can be seen that we all have specific comprehension problems at certain times, although fortunately these are rather rare for most of us. For others however, such comprehension failures can be the rule rather than the exception, and it is the source of these general comprehension problems which we will attempt to clarify in this chapter. Before dealing further with the possible reasons for specific comprehension disabilities, it may help to look first at the nature of the reading comprehension process.

Comprehension as reader-text interaction

In a real sense, reading comprehension is the end product of a communication process. This communication process involves the transmission of ideas from the author to the reader using the medium of the written text. In producing the written text, the author has certain knowledge to communicate which he or she believes the reader does not have. However, the reader is likely to have at least some prior knowledge of the subject the author is writing about. Therefore, the author has to produce a text which both assumes what the reader already knows about the subject and conveys the new knowledge the author wishes to communicate. If the author wrongly assumes that the reader has some prior knowledge of the subject matter which he does not have, the text will be difficult to comprehend. For example, in writing this book I have assumed that the typical reader will have little or no knowledge of research methods or statistics. If I had assumed such prior knowledge on the part of the reader, the book would not have been fully comprehensible to the type of reader for which it is intended. What is perhaps more surprising is that if the author assumes too little prior knowledge and states everything in explicit detail, the reader may again have comprehension difficulties because the text is found to be either boring or confusing. Legal documents are a very good example of this phenomenon. In order to avoid legal disputes, these documents attempt to make everything completely explicit, whereas normally writers leave obvious points implicit and assume the reader will correctly infer them from prior knowledge.

Not only does an author have to make assumptions about his readership's prior knowledge of the subject matter, but also about their vocabulary, language competence, and memory limitations. Again, any inappropriate assumptions on the part of the author may lead to comprehension difficulties. The general point being made is that authors tailor their writing to suit a particular readership and their work may not necessarily be appropriate to other readers having different background knowledge, vocabulary, language competence, or memory limitations. In other words, whether or not a particular piece of text can be comprehended depends on the interaction between the demands of the text and the resources of the reader. Whenever the text fails to match the reader, comprehension problems will occur. For example, if a child reads a text which was written for adults, virtually all of the writer's assumptions about his readership will be inappropriate and comprehension difficulties will result for numerous reasons. Other such reader-text mismatches were occurring in the instances of comprehension failure we discussed earlier – namely reading technical material and foreign language texts. Although all readers will have difficulties with some texts because these fail to match their resources, other readers may be generally lacking in some cognitive resource so that comprehension problems are more the rule than the exception. These readers have general difficulties in comprehending written materials which might be considered appropriate for them in terms of word identification demands.

The levels at which comprehension difficulties arise

Comprehension failures can occur because of problems at any of a number of levels. We will briefly discuss each one of these levels as a forerunner to a more detailed treatment of each later on. The distinctions between the various levels of the comprehension process adopted here follow broadly the work of Kintsch and van Dijk (1978).

A first level where difficulties can occur is in the conversion of the sentences of a text into their underlying ideas. For example, the sentence *Old Nino ate the pizza slowly* contains three basic ideas which the reader must extract. These ideas can be expressed roughly as (1) *Nino ate the pizza.* (2) *Nino is old.* (3) *The eating was slow.* These same ideas might have been expressed in other ways in the text. One other way would be *The pizza was eaten slowly by old Nino.* The psychological processes involved when readers convert written sentences into basic ideas (and writers convert ideas into written sentences) are very complex and nowhere near fully understood.

The second level at which comprehension problems could arise is in the organisation of the ideas expressed in a text according to their interrelationships. This level is a little difficult to appreciate, but can be understood better by considering what happens when the sentences in a newspaper article are scrambled as in the following example:

> The cadets, ranging in age from 11 to 18 years, will be wearing their uniforms and collecting from the city and outer areas. But on the weekend, 22 Flotilla 8 cadets and their parents will rattle those cans in the hope of raising enough money for a training boat which will also be used for rescue. They are providing a totally voluntary service, receiving no support from any organisation except the work they do themselves. Normally it is the Coastguards who come to the aid of distressed craft on and

> around Corio Bay. The Flotilla 8 Coastguard Cadets will turn the tables and ask for help in Friday night and Saturday morning.

Although it is possible to extract the ideas from each individual sentence, the passage is difficult to comprehend because the reader cannot easily organise these ideas in a coherent way. For example, the first sentence of the scrambled passage makes mention of 'cadets' who are 'collecting'. This sentence presupposes that the reader knows who the cadets are and what they are collecting, but the sentences which supply this knowledge do not come till later in the passage. The reader may have to reread the scrambled passage several times to grasp the interrelationships between the ideas, compared with the single reading which would be required for the original unscrambled version.

A third level at which comprehension problems can occur is in relating the information expressed in the text to the reader's previous knowledge of any subject they read about. The more previous knowledge a reader has, the easier will it be to assimilate the new ideas expressed in the text. As we have discussed previously, authors always assume a certain degree of background knowledge on the part of their readership. Readers who do not have the background knowledge assumed by the author, or who fail to utilise what previous knowledge they have, will experience comprehension problems.

Bransford and Johnson (1973) have devised a passage which provides a good illustration of the importance of background knowledge to comprehension:

> The procedure is actually quite simple. First you arrange things into different groups. Of course, one pile may be sufficient depending on how much there is to do. If you have to go somewhere else due to lack of facilities that is the next step, otherwise you are pretty well set. It is important not to overdo things. That is, it is better to do too few things at once than too many. In the short run this may not seem important but complications can easily arise. A mistake can be expensive as well. At first the whole procedure will seem complicated. Soon, however, it will become just another facet of life. It is difficult to foresee any end to the necessity for this task in the immediate future, but then one never can tell. After the procedure is completed one arranges the materials into different groups again.

> Then they can be put into their appropriate places. Eventually they will be used once more and the whole cycle will then have to be repeated. However, that is part of life (p. 400).

This passage is fairly incomprehensible until we are told that the title of the passage is '*Washing Clothes*.' Without this title we are in exactly the same position as somebody who completely lacked background knowledge of washing clothes. Although we do, in fact, possess the relevant knowledge in this case, the passage is written in such a way that we do not know to bring this knowledge to bear on it. Consequently, we function just like a reader who lacked the relevant knowledge altogether.

A final level at which comprehension problems can occur is in the extraction of the most important ideas from the wealth of detail usually provided in a text. For example, if somebody reads a lengthy text, such as a play, they generally have no difficulty in giving a short summary of the plot if they have comprehended it adequately. However, to generate an appropriate summary a reader has to be able to discriminate the important ideas from the less important and only include the former in the summary. For example, a reader who summarises *Macbeth* as being 'about the downfall of a king who came to the throne by committing murder' has managed to condense the contents of the play considerably and yet has still retained the essence of the plot. On the other hand, a reader who summarises it as being 'about some witches' prophesies and how they come true' has certainly managed to condense the ideas of the play but could be said to have missed the major theme. In the long term, we tend to retain in memory only the major parts of what we read. The ability to select out these ideas and to condense the text accordingly is an important aspect of reading comprehension.

Having briefly distinguished various levels at which comprehension difficulties may occur, let us examine each of them in more detail.

Extracting ideas from written sentences

We have seen that comprehension difficulties might plausibly occur in the process of converting written sentences into their underlying ideas. Several pieces of evidence indicate that there are indeed readers who characteristically have problems with this process. For example, a study by Isakson and Miller (1976) investigated the reading of fourth graders who had adequate word-recognition skills but deficient comprehension. They attempted to show that these children are not sensitive to the language constraints of sentences they read. Isakson and Miller's experiment involved the children reading examples of three types of sentences. The first type were meaningful sentences such as *The old farmer planted the bean seeds in the rich, brown soil.* Sentences of the second type had a transitive verb in them which made them meaningless, while still following the rules of English syntax; for example, *The old farmer paid the bean seeds in the rich, brown soil.* Sentences of the third type had an intransitive verb which made them meaningless and also violated normal syntax; for example, *The old farmer went the bean seeds in the rich, brown soil.*

If a child reading such meaningless sentences aloud is also extracting the underlying ideas, he will have difficulties when he encounters the anomalous verbs. For example, the child who reads *The farmer went,* and understands the idea communicated in this phrase, will be expecting to learn where the farmer went to. The child might make the error of saying *The farmer went to,* before correcting himself and reading *the bean seeds.* On the other hand, a child who is reading the sentences word for word and not extracting the underlying ideas will be undaunted by the meaninglessness of what he is reading. Such a child would be unlikely to make meaning-preserving errors in his reading.

Isakson and Miller indeed found that normal readers (those with both adequate word recognition and comprehension skills) made more errors when reading the meaningless sentences aloud than when reading normal sentences. These children were especially disrupted when reading the sentences which were meaningless and violated normal syntax. However, the children with a comprehension disability made errors with much the same frequency whether reading aloud meaningful or meaningless sentences. In other words, the children with a comprehension disability failed to make use of the language constraints of the sentences they were reading.

Cromer (1970) has shown that adults with adequate word identification skills but poor comprehension also have problems in extracting the ideas expressed in a text. In his study, Cromer compared these adults to good comprehenders in the reading of stories. (The study also looked at adults with both poor word identification skills and poor comprehension, but this aspect of the study is not directly relevant to the present topic and will be omitted.)

The stories used in the study were printed in four different ways.

The first way was for the sentences of the story to be printed in normal fashion and presented one at a time. The sentences looked like the following example:

The cow jumped over the moon.

The second way involved the stories being printed as a series of single words which were presented one at a time:

The
cow
jumped
over
the
moon.

This method of presenting the stories would be expected to encourage word by word reading at the expense of extracting the underlying ideas. The third way involved presenting the sentences so that each meaningful phrase was distinguished. This method was expected to facilitate the extraction of meaning since the sentences were organised in terms of ideas. An example is:

The cow jumped   over the moon.

The fourth way was to group words of a sentence together in a way which did not make sense. For example:

The cow   jumped over the   moon.

After each story was read, the adults had to answer a series of questions which tested their comprehension. Cromer was interested in assessing how the four different methods of presenting the stories would affect comprehension for the two groups of readers. As would be expected, the adults with a comprehension disability were poorer at understanding the stories where the sentences were printed normally. When the stories were presented one word at a time, the adults with a comprehension disability performed at much the same level as when full sentence presentation was used. This result would be expected of readers who process text on a word-by-word basis rather than focussing on the extraction of meaning. However, the good comprehenders were greatly disadvantaged by the word-at-a-time presentation of the stories and comprehended much less. Perhaps the most interesting finding emerged when the sentences of the stories were grouped into meaningful phrases. This way of presenting the stories led to large increases in the performance of the disabled comprehenders and they in fact comprehended as well as the good comprehenders. Evidently, the phrase groupings helped the disabled comprehenders to extract ideas from the text in the way that good comprehenders do normally. Grouping into meaningless phrases, on the other hand, did not help the performance of the disabled comprehenders and had an adverse effect on the good comprehenders, presumably because it conflicted with their natural tendencies.

The effects of grouping into meaningful phrases has not been investigated in younger readers who have a comprehension disability. However, a study by Levin (1973) has looked at the effects on fourth grade children of another technique for inducing comprehension. The technique involved having the children form mental images of the contents of each sentence while they were reading a story. It was found that children with good word recognition skills but poor comprehension could improve their performance considerably when using this technique. It seems that forming images for each sentence induced these children to attend to the ideas present in the stories rather than just read word by word. However, although this technique aided children with a comprehension disability when they were reading stories, it is probably not of any practical value in reading more abstract materials. For example, it would be well-nigh impossible to form mental images of the contents of this book because of the relatively abstract nature of the ideas being presented.

Organising ideas in a coherent pattern

Having extracted the ideas from sentences, the reader must then organise them into a coherent pattern to appreciate how they relate together. As an example, let us look at how the ideas expressed in a brief passage might be organised. The ideas expressed in the following passage might be roughly expressed by the groups of words which have been bracketed off.

> (The island of Tasmania) (lies off) (the south east coast) (of the Australian continent.) (Every summer) (hordes of tourists) (come to) (the state) (attracted by) (its natural beauty.)

If we consider the ideas in this passage, we will see that each one is generally related in some manner to another idea in the passage. We could express the relationships between the ideas of the first sentence as follows:

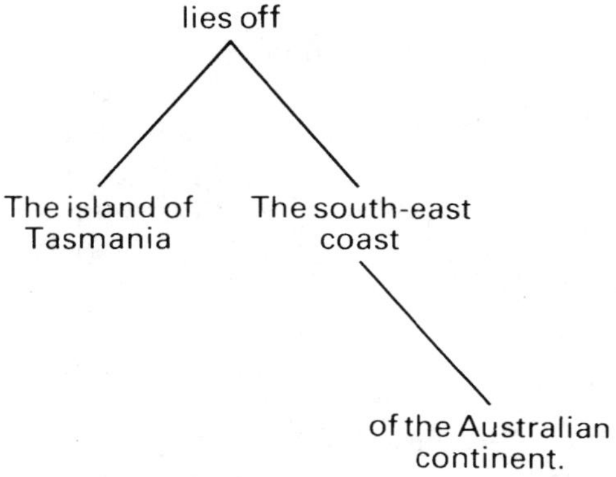

In other words, the idea *lies off* appears to provide a link between *the island of Tasmania* and *the south-east coast. The south-east coast* is then linked to *of the Australian continent.*

Let us now look at how the ideas of the second sentence might be organised:

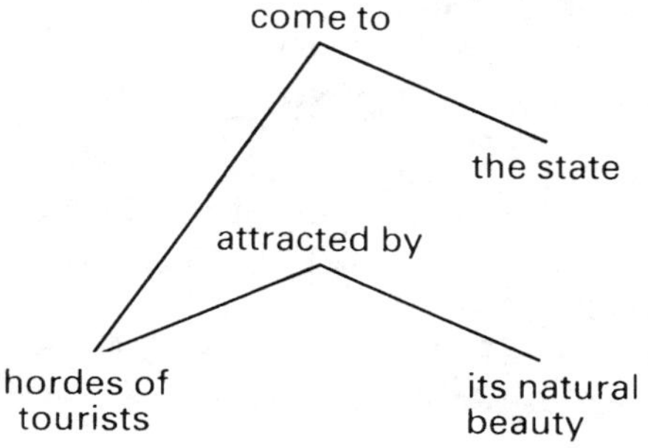

Again, each idea appears to be directly linked to other ideas. Next, the ideas of the second sentence have to be linked to those of the first sentence if the organisation of ideas in the whole passage is to be appreciated. However, there is a problem about making this linkage. There is no *direct* linkage between the ideas of the second sentence and those of the first. Readers familiar with the island of Tasmania will of course know that it is also a state and will therefore realise that these two ideas are linked. However, this linkage requires an inference based on the reader's background knowledge of the topic. Somebody reading this passage without having the background knowledge that Tasmania is a state would have difficulty making this inference and might have trouble organising the ideas into the pattern intended by the author. For example, an ignorant reader might incorrectly suppose that Australia was the state being referred to, rather than Tasmania.

The general point of this example is to illustrate that there are often gaps in the links between ideas expressed in a text and that these must be filled by inferences based on general world knowledge. Any reader who either lacks the relevant world knowledge or has problems in using it to draw such inferences will be unable to organise the ideas expressed in a text into a coherent pattern. Such a reader will inevitably have problems comprehending the meaning of the passage. However, background knowledge has an importance to reading which goes far beyond the process of drawing inferences to maintain the coherence of ideas in a text.

Role of knowledge frames in comprehension

When people read a text they organise together all the ideas presented on a particular subject and relate these ideas to their previous knowledge of the subject. When a particular idea is encountered in the text the reader pulls out a packet of appropriate knowledge from his long-term memory and relates the incoming ideas to that knowledge. We will refer to these packets of knowledge about a subject as *knowledge frames*. Knowledge frames provide a sort of mental scaffolding on which the reader can construct the meaning of a text. It may help to make the notion of knowledge frames more concrete by looking at a particular example. Take the following passage about Christmas:

A Family Christmas

> Judy was very excited that it was Christmas Eve. She hung her stocking by the fireplace and attached a note to Santa Claus

> asking for the trumpet she wanted so badly. Judy longed for the night to pass quickly. She could think of nothing but the trumpet she would have in the morning. Meanwhile, Judy's mother and father were busy in the kitchen preparing goodies for the Christmas Day dinner. It was expected to be a typical hot Christmas Day, so the family planned to have Christmas dinner on the beach.

The title of this passage would activate the knowledge frame for Christmas in most readers. This knowledge frame might contain general information about the religious significance of Christmas, typical Christmas traditions, and the time of year when it occurs. The specific ideas presented in the passage can then be related to this knowledge frame. For example, when the part of the passage about a note to Santa Claus is encountered, the reader will realise that Santa Claus is supposed to come down the chimney the night before Christmas and leave presents in a stocking for the children of a household. Anyone who did not have this background knowledge would be at a loss to understand the passage. The reader will also use the information in the Christmas knowledge frame to make reasonable inferences about the characters and events described in the passage. For example, most readers would infer that Judy is a pre-adolescent girl, because it is generally known that only young children believe in Santa Claus and hang out a stocking in the hope of getting a present.

Once a knowledge frame is activated it not only aids interpretation of what has been read but leads the reader to anticipate that certain sorts of other ideas might be presented. If the reader's expectations are not met, there may be comprehension problems. For example, in the Family Christmas passage the reference to 'a typical hot Christmas Day' may have produced problems of this sort for some readers. The Christmas knowledge frames of many people would contain information that Christmas occurs in winter and is often associated with snow. Thus, the reader of the passage is primed to interpret the events in terms of cold weather and possibly snow. Any reference to hot weather might cause the reader to do one of a number of things: conclude that the passage does not make sense; suspect that a vital point has been missed and reread the passage to look for it; or imagine some circumstance where hot weather could occur at Christmas, such as a freak air current blowing from the tropics. Other readers will have no problem at all, because their knowledge frame contains information that Christmas occurs in winter only in the Northern Hemisphere. In the Southern Hemisphere it occurs in summer. A reader with this knowledge will correctly infer that the events described in the passage are occurring in the Southern Hemisphere. The reader might have been primed to make this inference if the passage had been given a title such as *A Family Christmas in Australia.* This title might have activated an Australia knowledge frame as well as a Christmas knowledge frame. The reader's Australia knowledge frame would plausibly contain the information that Australia is in the Southern Hemisphere and therefore has the reverse seasons to the Northern Hemisphere, even if the Christmas frame itself did not contain any information about the Southern Hemisphere. In this instance, the passage would be more readily comprehended.

To sum up so far, background knowledge is important to reading comprehension in two ways. First, it allows the reader to make inferences which can fill in gaps in the links between ideas in a text. Second, it provides a sort of mental scaffolding to help the reader interpret the information present in a text. Therefore, a lack of relevant background knowledge would explain the difficulties many people have in understanding certain specific texts. An example of this phenomenon, mentioned earlier, was of the layman attempting to read a technical book written for a specialist readership. However, if a reader has limited background knowledge across a wide variety of areas, there will be general difficulties in comprehending what is read.

Dealing with comprehension failure

At some time or other all readers are faced with the situation where they fail to understand some part of a text. When skilled readers fail to comprehend, they will generally take some sort of remedial action to overcome the problem. They may slow down their rate of reading, allocate more time and effort to understanding a difficult point, reread an earlier part of the text in an effort to clarify their confusion, skip ahead in the text to see whether information introduced by the author later on aids understanding, or consult a dictionary, encyclopedia or expert for further background information on the particular point. However, in order to use these remedial strategies, the reader has to first be aware that he or she is not fully understanding the author's message. It seems counterintuitive that someone could read a text and yet not realise that they are not fully understanding it. However, studies have shown that young children can fail to understand something but still believe that they do understand it.

A study by Markman (1977) illustrates this phenomenon quite well. Markman told young children from Grades 1-3 that she was writing some instructions for a card game and a magic trick. These instructions were meant to be suitable for young children and she needed their advice on the clarity and completeness of the instructions. By having the children act as consultants to advise her on the adequacy of the instructions, Markman hoped that they would be quite willing to admit that they could not understand. The actual instructions were written so that they were incomplete and could not possibly be understood by anyone. For example, the instructions for the card game were as follows:

> We each put our cards in a pile. We both turn over the top card in our pile. We look at the cards to see who has the special card. Then we turn over the next card in our pile to see who has the special card this time. In the end the person with the most cards wins the game.

These instructions are inadequate in a number of ways. For instance, there is no mention of what the special card is. When the instructions were read to the children, and they were asked whether there were any inadequacies, more third graders than first graders realised that some vital information was missing. In fact, most first graders only realised that the instructions were inadequate when they were actually asked to carry them out and play the game. In other words, the first graders were not aware that their understanding of the game was faulty.

A similar phenomenon may occur when some children read. They may fail to understand and yet not realise it. In such instances, the child will fail to take the necessary remedial action which may have helped overcome the comprehension failure. The process by which readers assess whether or not they are understanding is known as *comprehension monitoring*. It has been suggested that poor comprehenders may sometimes have problems because they fail to adequately monitor their own understanding.

Some recent research by Garner (1980) has looked into the possibility that poor comprehenders tend to be unaware of their own lack of understanding. Garner compared the comprehension monitoring of good and poor comprehenders from the seventh and eighth grades. Garner's method of studying comprehension monitoring was to have the children read passages which contained obvious inconsistencies and see whether they could be detected. She took some simple passages about American heroes from a reader for fifth grade children. These passages were divided into four sections. The first and third sections were completely sensible but the second and fourth were altered so as to contain inconsistencies. For example, one passage was about Thomas Jefferson and discussed his work to systematise the coinage. An inconsistency was introduced into the passage by altering the word *numbers* to *letters* in a passage about numbers, counting, and the establishment of a money system. The altered sentence read *In some primitive time early people had invented a system of letters.* Although this sentence was perfectly reasonable in itself, it did not make sense in the context of the paragraph. Garner told the children that these passages were written for a textbook and she wanted to find out whether they were easy to understand or whether the writers would have to make some changes. The children were asked to read each section of a passage and classify it as *very easy, OK,* or *difficult to understand.* If a child did not find a section of a passage very easy to understand, he or she was asked why it was unclear. What Garner found was that the good comprehenders classified the inconsistent sections as being harder to understand than the consistent ones. They made comments like: *I don't see what letters have to do with what Jefferson was doing.* In other words, they were aware that they were not fully understanding what they were reading. However, the poor comprehenders classified all the sections in pretty much the same way, irrespective of whether they contained inconsistencies. Even when they did feel that they could understand what they had read, the poor comprehenders did not comment on the inconsistencies present in the passages. Instead they make comments like: *The words were longer, I didn't like that part as well,* or *I didn't understand why he wanted to go to the Pole.* In short, it appears that these children may sometimes be worse at monitoring their comprehension than are good comprehenders. They may therefore fail to take appropriate remedial action when they are not comprehending what they are reading.

The types of remedial action which skilled readers may take when they fail to comprehend became evident in a study by Baker (1979). Baker had university students read passages which contained confusions and afterwards asked them whether they had noticed these confusions. To give an example of a confusion, one passage about the Incas stated that their economy was extremely backward for its time. However, the passage then went on to say that their farming methods were quite sophisticated, that everybody paid taxes, and that unemployment was virtually absent. Baker found that the students noticed only 23 per cent of the confusions while they were reading, and even when explicitly asked to search for them could only detect 38 per cent. However, the reason that these skilled adult readers failed to report the confusions was that they automatically carried out procedures for resolving the problems caused by the confusions. Baker describes the remedial strategies used by the skilled readers as follows:

> A common response upon first encountering a confusion was to reread previously read information, checking to see if some crucial bit of information had been overlooked. Another strategy was to make a mental note that a problem had occurred, but to continue reading in the hope that clarification would occur later in the text. Since readers have a right to expect clarity from an author, this is an adaptive strategy. The reader who becomes bogged down in a confusing section of text that could have been clarified with continued reading is technically a comprehension monitor, but in this case is not employing an effective repair strategy.
>
> Once the subjects established that a confusion existed, they often drew upon prior knowledge to render the text more comprehensible. They would decide that some relevant information had not been included in the text and then would make an inference to bridge the gap. However, sometimes subjects realized there was a problem but decided it was trivial and not worth the effort of trying to resolve.

In order to use strategies of this sort, readers have to first realise that they are not making sense of what they are reading. Without this realisation, they will plough merrily along through the text and not gain a full understanding.

Producing summaries

After skilled readers have read a text, they can easily produce a summary of its contents. In fact, they can easily produce a whole range of summaries which vary in length and detail. At one extreme is a summary which contains all the detail the reader can recall and at the other extreme is a summary which consists only of a statement of the general topic of the text. For example, a child asked to summarise *The Three Bears* might give a very brief summary, something like the following:

> It's about a girl who visits the three bears' house while they are out and uses all their things.

Alternatively, a child might give a more detailed summary such as:

> It's about a girl called Goldilocks who goes into the three bears' house while they are out for a walk. She tastes their porridge, sits on their chairs, and tries their beds. She falls asleep on one of the beds and the Three Bears come home. They see that somebody has been eating their porridge, and sitting on their chairs. They go into the bedroom and find Goldilocks asleep. She wakes up, gets a fright when she sees them, and runs away.

How do readers go about reducing the ideas in a text to produce summaries such as these? Kintsch and van Dijk (1978) have argued that we apply certain summarisation rules to the ideas we read and that these produce the summary. They have distinguished four such rules. These four summarisation rules are not consciously learned and applied. Rather they are used automatically and unconsciously by the skilled reader.

1 *The Deletion Rule.* This rule removes any irrelevant content. It might be applied to the following passage by deleting the sentence *The Opera House looked really beautiful in the moonlight.*

> Yesterday I went to the Sydney Opera House to hear a concert. The Opera House looked really beautiful in the moonlight. The concert started late, so I bought myself a snack to eat in the restaurant. The snack gave me a stomach ache, so I did not enjoy the concert at all. It is the last time I will buy anything at that restaurant.

2 *The Integration Rule.* This rule removes redundant ideas. For example, the very first sentence can serve as an adequate summary

of the following passage because the rest simply says the same thing in more detail.

> John had his lunch. He had a bowl of French onion soup with some wholemeal bread, followed by a carob milkshake and a large Granny Smith apple.

3 *The Generalisation Rule.* This rule substitutes a general category name for a list of instances of the category. For example, *The whole family was working* becomes the summary for:

> Mum was cleaning the car. Dad was washing the dishes. The children were doing their homework.

4 *The Construction Rule.* This rule summarises a sequence of actions or events by a term that covers the whole sequence. For example, the following passage might be summarised as *Zoe studied for her exam.*

> Zoe went to the library early on Tuesday morning. She took along all her textbooks and class notes. She read them all and then reread them. She tested herself by writing summaries of what she had read. She located some old exam papers on a shelf in the library and attempted to do the questions. By the end of the day, Zoe felt confident she could pass the exam.

By applying these summarisation rules again and again to the ideas in a text, the reader arrives at progressively shorter summaries of its contents, until ultimately only a statement of the general topic of the text is left. Basically, the reader eliminates the details and retains the important ideas. However, in order to eliminate details and retain important ideas, the reader has to have some criterion for assessing what parts of the text are important and what are unimportant. If a reader produced a summary by applying summarisation rules at random, without any overriding direction, he would produce a somewhat bizarre result which would undoubtedly fail to convey the flavour of the original text to anyone else.

What is it then that defines which parts of a text are more important than others? The importance of various parts of a text is defined by the reader's goals and purposes. By adopting a particular purpose in reading a text, the reader sets up expectations that certain types of information will be found. A reader who reads a text with one purpose in mind will be seeking out different kinds of information than a reader who has a different purpose. This point is very well illustrated by the results of some experiments by Pichert and Anderson (1977). These researchers constructed passages which could be viewed from two perspectives. The importance of the various ideas in the passages differed for each of the perspectives. One of the stories was about two boys who were playing hooky from school, and went as follows:

> The two boys ran until they came to the driveway, 'See, I told you today was good for skipping school,' said Mark. 'Mom is never home on Thursday,' he added. Tall hedges hid the house from the road so the pair strolled across the finely landscaped yard. 'I never knew your place was so big,' said Pete. 'Yeah, but it's nicer now than it used to be since Dad had the new stone siding put on and added the fireplace.'
>
> There were front and back doors and a side door which led to the garage which was empty except for three parked 10-speed bikes. They went in the side door, Mark explaining that it was always open in case his younger sisters got home earlier than their mother.
>
> Pete wanted to see the house so Mark started with the living room. It, like the rest of the downstairs, was newly painted. Mark turned on the stereo, the noise of which worried Pete. 'Don't worry, the nearest house is a quarter of a mile away,' Mark shouted. Pete felt more comfortable observing that no houses could be seen in any direction beyond the huge yard.
>
> The dining room, with all the china, silver and cut glass, was no place to play so the boys moved into the kitchen where they made sandwiches. Mark said they wouldn't go to the basement because it had been damp and musty ever since the new plumbing had been installed.
>
> 'This is where my Dad keeps his famous paintings and his coin collection,' Mark said as they peered into the den. Mark bragged that he could get spending money whenever he needed it since he'd discovered that his Dad kept a lot in the desk drawer.
>
> There were three upstairs bedrooms. Mark showed Pete his mother's closet which was filled with furs and the locked box which held her jewels. His sister's room was uninteresting except

> for the color TV which Mark carried to his room. Mark bragged that the bathroom in the hall was his since one had been added to his sister's room for their use. The big highlight in his room, though, was a leak in the ceiling where the old roof had finally rotted.

University students were asked to read this passage from one of two perspectives, that of a potential homebuyer or that of a burglar, and to assess the importance of the various ideas in the passage from the perspective they had been given. For example, from a homebuyer's perspective it is important to know that the downstairs rooms had been recently painted, that the basement was damp, and that there was a leak in the ceiling. However, from the other perspective these points are unimportant. It would be of more interest to a burglar to know that there were 10-speed bikes in the garage, collections of paintings and coins in the den, and a color TV in a bedroom. Pichert and Anderson indeed found that readers who were asked to approach the passage from the homebuyer's perspective regarded entirely different ideas as important from readers who approached it from the burglar's perspective. In a subsequent experiment, Pichert and Anderson had university students read the passage from either the homebuyer or burglar perspective and later tested their recall of the ideas in the passage. They found that the readers who read the passage from the burglar's perspective had a greater tendency to recall those ideas which were of importance to a burglar. Conversely, readers who read it from a potential homebuyer's perspective had a greater tendency to recall the ideas which were of importance to a homebuyer. In other words, the readers' goals and purposes during reading influence which ideas in a passage they regard as important and consequently which ideas they are most likely to recall subsequently.

Although different readers may approach a particular text with different purposes, as in Pichert and Anderson's study, there are many occasions when a text is approached from the same perspective by most readers. For example, certain types of texts have a highly conventional structure familiar to most people who read them. These conventional structures may provide a basis for determining which ideas in a text are more important. For example, traditional European folk stories and fables usually follow a conventional structure, as do many children's stories. This conventional story structure is often referred to as a *story schema*. For example, Stein and Nezworski

(1978) see the story schema as consisting of a Setting, Initiating Event, Internal Response, Attempt, Consequence and Reaction. The following story fits this schema perfectly and provides an example of each of the story components.

Setting	Once there was a big gray fish named Albert who lived in a big icy pond near the edge of a forest.
Initiating event	One day, Albert was swimming around the pond when he spotted a big juicy worm on top of the water.
Internal Response	Albert knew how delicious worms tasted and wanted to eat that one for his dinner.
Attempt	So he swam very close to the worm and bit into him.
Consequence	Suddenly, Albert was pulled through the water into a boat. He had been caught by a fisherman.
Reaction	Albert felt sad and wished he had been more careful.

From hearing many, many stories which fit this schema, children in European cultures learn that stories tend to consist of these various components arranged in a particular order. When producing summaries they can use this schema as a basis for including the most important ideas. For example, a good summary of a story should retain each of the components of the story schema. If one of the components were left out from a summary, it would not retain the essential character of the original story.

Although stories arising out of European culture may follow a schema of the sort described by Stein and Nezworski, stories from other cultures may follow their own very different schema. For example, in some American Indian cultures the story schema follows a principle of fours, in that there are four episodes, four actors using four instruments, and so on. Knowledge of this schema aids comprehension and recall of American Indian stories just as knowledge of the story schema with which we are more familiar aids comprehension and recall of stories from a European cultural tradition. However, someone familiar with the European story schema will not be able to apply it successfully to American Indian stories and so will not be able to produce good summaries for these stories. A study by Kintsch and Greene (1978) showed that this was the case by having university students read some European stories and some Apache stories and afterwards produce summaries of them. They found that the students produced much poorer summaries of the Apache stories than of the European stories. Being unfamiliar with the story schema for Apache stories, the students were unable to pick out the most important ideas in these stories for their summaries.

Having briefly looked at the cognitive processes involved in producing summaries of what has been read, let us now return to the issue of reading comprehension disabilities. General problems in producing adequate summaries after reading a text might arise from two sources. Firstly, a reader might not be using the full set of summarisation rules. Some of these rules (e.g., the Construction Rule) appear to be very difficult to apply, but an adequate summary cannot be produced without them. A second source of problems in producing summaries lies with the reader's goals and purposes. A reader who characteristically approaches a text from an unusual perspective will also produce unusual summaries. As we have seen, certain types of text have a conventional structure which aids the reading of somebody who is familiar with it. A reader who lacks a knowledge of conventional structures like the story schema will have difficulty in selecting out the more important ideas for a summary. Very little research has been carried out on summarisation problems and the little that has been done has focussed on problems in using summarisation rules.

One study, by Brown and Day (1980), looked at the ability of readers of various ages to use summarisation rules. They studied summarisation in children from Grades 5, 7, and 10 as well as in various college students. Even the youngest children were found to be very good at using summarisation rules which involved deleting irrelevant or redundant material. With the other more difficult rules, on the other hand, there were marked age differences, with the older students using them more often. However, even the college students frequently did not use the Construction Rule when it was appropriate. In other words, they found it very difficult to make up a topic sentence to describe a whole sequence of events. A group of college students who were remedial studiers performed only at the level of seventh graders, and were only able to effectively use the summarisation rules involving deletion of material. It therefore appears that difficulty in using certain summarisation rules is a source of comprehension problems. The greatest difficulty seems to arise when summarisation requires the reader to add information not explicitly contained in the text rather than to delete or manipulate information already provided by the author.

A subsequent study by Day (1980) attempted to train American junior college students to use summarisation rules and to check that they were using them appropriately. Some of these students were normal readers and writers; others were of normal reading ability, but had writing problems. With these students, Day tried out various types of instruction which varied in their degree of explicitness. In the least explicit type of instruction the students were told to produce a summary by concentrating on the main ideas and eliminating the trivial points, but they were not taught any methods for doing this. In the most explicit type of instruction, the students were trained in how to use the various summarisation rules and were also taught to check how well they had applied these rules. Although all the types of instruction had an effect, the most explicit form of instruction produced the greatest effect. Furthermore, the students who were normal readers and writers benefitted more from the instruction and required less explicit instruction than those who were normal readers but poor writers. The results of Day's training study are certainly encouraging, but we must be careful not to be overly optimistic about the effectiveness of training in summarisation. Day was certainly able to improve students' ability to produce summaries for very short passages by having them consciously apply all of the summarisation rules she had taught. However, we must remember that summarisation rules are normally applied automatically and unconsciously while we read. A skilled reader will easily be able to produce a short summary of Tolstoy's novel *War and Peace* even though it took several months to read. However, it might take a good part of a life-time to produce a summary of *War and Peace* by working through it sentence by sentence and deliberately applying some summarisation rules learned by explicit instruction. It would be very difficult, and perhaps even impossible, to train students to carry out summarisation effortlessly and automatically during the reading process itself.

Conclusion

The study of reading comprehension has a very recent history, having been ignored as too difficult a problem until the 1970s. However, our knowledge of the subject is now increasing very rapidly. With greater theoretical understanding of reading comprehension will come greater understanding of comprehension disabilities. Although comparatively little research has been done on comprehension disabilities to this point in time, we can expect to see great advances in this area in the years to come. In this chapter, we have seen how notions of the component processes involved in reading comprehension can illuminate our understanding of the likely sources of comprehension disabilities.

7 Spelling disabilities

It is usually the case that people with reading difficulties also have trouble with spelling. This is not really surprising because reading and spelling are related skills and one would intuitively expect people who are poor at one to be poor at the other. Indeed, there is generally found to be a strong correlation between the two abilities when tests of reading and spelling are given to a large group of people.

What is surprising is that spelling difficulties are sometimes present in people with apparently normal or even superior reading ability. One sometimes sees a specific problem of this sort in university students and it can be a great disadvantage to them in writing essays and exam papers. Nevertheless, some of these students manage to achieve excellent academic records. It is certainly not unknown to find academics who are atrocious spellers and the problem no doubt exists in other professional groups as well. There are several ways in which the person with a specific spelling difficulty may attempt to circumvent the problem. Such a person may attempt to disguise the problem by poor handwriting, may avoid writing as much as possible, or may simply dismiss correct spelling as being arbitrary and an unnecessary restriction imposed by schoolteachers. Perhaps the most successful way to avoid the problem is for the poor speller to secure a secretary who can spell correctly and type any written material he or she produces, but this is a solution generally open only to those who have already succeeded in spite of their spelling difficulty.

Although spelling difficulties can occur in people of all ages, virtually all the research on the subject has been carried out with children. For this reason, the remainder of this chapter will be confined to a discussion of the understanding we have gained from research on spelling difficulties in children.

The spelling process

Before examining spelling difficulties in detail, it is worth digressing to consider the sort of processes that go on when we spell a word. First of all consider how we spell highly familiar words like our name, or highly irregular words like *through, tough,* or *rhythm.* It seems likely that we have the spellings of these words stored in some sort of mental lexicon and can look them up when required. In fact, a spelling mechanism based around a mental lexicon is essential if we are to spell irregular words at all. When we describe these words as having irregular spellings, we mean that they cannot be spelled purely by the use of rules relating sound to print. In fact, if there were no mechanism for looking up the spellings of words in a mental lexicon, it is doubtful that we could handle English spelling particularly well. There are simply too many words which cannot be correctly spelled using sound-to-print conversion rules. The limitation of spelling rules becomes apparent when a computer is programmed to spell purely by this mechanism. Hanna, Hanna, Hodges and Rudorf (1966) programmed a computer to spell by using over 300 spelling rules, but the program did not perform particularly well. It was given 17,000 different words to spell and failed with over half of them. Some of the computer program's misspellings were:

Correct spelling	*Program's spelling*
BUS	BUSS
TEAM	TEEM
COAL	COLE
SWEET	SWEAT
TIE	TY

From these few examples, it can easily be seen that the program makes errors on quite common words which most children manage to spell without difficulty. Certainly, a well-educated adult would be able to spell correctly far more than 50 per cent of the 17,000 words attempted by the computer. It seems likely then that humans manage to be so successful at spelling by using information stored in a mental lexicon rather than relying purely on rules.

However, there are inevitably occasions when we wish to spell a word for which we do not have complete information stored in our mental lexicon. On such occasions, we need to use sound-to-print rules, or some related mechanism like spelling by analogy.

However, the use of rules in English spelling is by no means a simple process. Consider, for example, the following possible spelling rules:

> The sound /t/ is written as *t* or *tt*.
> The sound /k/ is written as *c, k, ck* or *ch*.
> the sound /s/ is written as *s, c,* or *ss*.

The interesting thing to notice about English sound-to-print rules, is that most sounds can plausibly be represented several different ways in print. To take a concrete example, the word *cat* might also be written as *katt* or *kat*. And similarly, *gear* could be written as *gere* or *geer*. If we are to spell correctly using rules, we obviously need some method of selecting the appropriate letters to represent each sound.

In English spelling, there are certain constraints which aid us in this selection. For example, the position of a sound in a word influences the way it is written. The word *cat* could not be written as *ckat* because *ck* never occurs at the beginning of words. However, in the word *tack, ck* is a perfectly acceptable spelling for exactly the same sound. Another example of this phenomenon is the *ght* of *bight, bought, caught,* etc. It would be unacceptable to use this cluster of letters to represent a /t/ sound at the beginning of a word, although it is an acceptable alternative at the end of a word. It was only by ignoring positional constraints such as these that George Bernard Shaw was able to produce his celebrated spelling of *fish* as *ghoti* (from toug*h,* w*o*men, and atten*ti*on).

A second constraint on spelling is provided by the grammatical function of a word in a sentence. For example, *kicked* is not spelled *kickt,* even though this spelling would seem more appropriate on phonetic grounds, because *ed* indicates the verb is in the past tense. Similarly, *dogs* could be more appropriately spelled as *dogz* on phonetic grounds, but *s* is used to mark the plural of a noun in English spelling and *z* is not.

Yet another constraint is provided by the historical origin of a word. Many English words are of Germanic, Roman, or Greek origin. A particular sound may be spelled differently depending on the historical origin of the word in which it occurs. For example, in words derived from Greek, /k/ is written as *ch* (e.g., *chaos, cholera, psychology*), while in words of Roman origin it is written as *c* (e.g., *compose, concert, concord*). Of course, only an expert on the history of the English language would know the origins of words with any certainty, but the typical speller may have an intuitive knowledge that certain spellings are used in words with certain sound characteristics.

It can be seen that the print-to-sound rules which can be used in reading unfamiliar words are somewhat different in kind from the sound-to-print rules of spelling; the speller often has to make a choice between several plausible spellings, whereas the reader seldom has this problem. To take a simple example the reading of *cat* by print-to-sound rules is unambiguous because there is only one possible pronunciation. However, the spelling of *cat* is by no means so simple because the speller has several possible spellings to choose from (*cat, catt, kat*), each of which is plausible on phonetic grounds. Therefore, if spelling by rules is to be even marginally successful there needs to be some extra process involving the selection of the most appropriate alternative. We will refer to the constraints in English spelling which allow this selection to take place as *orthographic rules*.

The sort of processes that may go on in spelling are summarised in the diagram below:

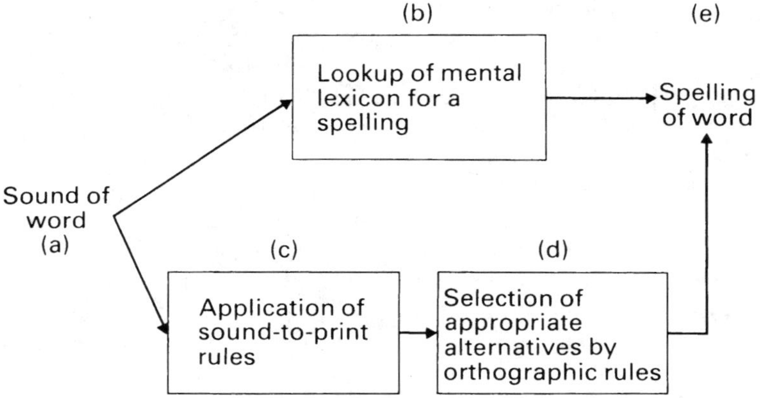

This diagram shows that when (a) a word has to be spelled we can achieve a spelling by either (b) looking up our mental lexicon to see whether a spelling for the word is stored there, or (c) apply sound-to-print rules to generate possible spellings and (d) select the most appropriate spelling from the options available using orthographic rules. Finally, whichever route is taken the result is (e) a spelling for the word. Although for ease of explanation, the diagram shows two separate routes for arriving at a spelling, these routes are unlikely to be completely separate. Both routes may be followed in parallel and they may interact with each other. To take an example, a person spelling the word *work* may only have in his lexicon the information that the vowel is spelled *o* rather than *e*, and the rest of the spelling (w rk) is generated using sound-to-print rules. In such a case, the speller is partly spelling the word using information in the lexicon, and partly using sound-to-print rules. Another way in which both strategies might be used in interaction is in spelling by analogy, as when the unknown word *yeast* is spelled by analogy with the known word *least*. In spelling by analogy, the spelling of a similar-sounding word is found in the lexicon, but a sound-to-print mechanism must be used to supply the spelling for the part of the unknown word which is different (e.g., the *y* of *yeast*).

Having briefly outlined a plausible model of the normal spelling process, let us now look at which components of this process are impaired in each of the types of spelling difficulties we distinguished earlier: reading-and-spelling retardation and spelling-only retardation. One clue to the nature of these spelling difficulties lies in the different types of spelling error which the two groups of spelling retardates make.

Types of spelling errors

One interesting way to classify spelling errors is as *phonetically accurate* or *phonetically inaccurate*. Some examples of these two types of spelling errors are:

Correct spelling	*Phonetically accurate misspelling*	*Phonetically inaccurate misspelling*
freeze	freez	frezze
resource	resorse	recourse
syllable	syllible	slibale

In making a phonetically inaccurate error, a child is obviously not using sound-to-print rules correctly. These misspellings are regarded as phonetically inaccurate because they could not be produced by a properly functioning sound-to-print mechanism. On the other hand, phonetically accurate errors reflect the successful use of a sound-

Table 7.1
Types of spelling errors made by different groups of spellers

Group of spellers	Number of children	Average age	Average IQ	Average reading age*	Average spelling age	% of phonetically inaccurate misspellings	% of phonetically accurate misspellings
Normal spellers	19	10.5	113	10.6	10.10	47	53
Spelling-only Retardates	4	9.8	108	10.2	8.1	57	43
Reading-and-spelling Retardates	19	10.2	111	8.2	7.10	75	25

Source: Adapted from Jorm, 1981.

*Note: A Reading Age of (say) 10.6 means that the child reads at the level of a child aged 10 years 6 months.

to-print mechanism, but the selection of inappropriate letters to represent the sounds of a word.

Several studies have shown that children with a spelling-only retardation differ from children with a reading-and-spelling retardation in the frequency with which they make these two types of spelling errors (Frith, 1980; Jorm, 1981; Nelson & Warrington, 1974). Table 7.1 shows some typical results. As can be seen from the Table, the spelling-only retardates make more phonetically-accurate errors than the reading-and-spelling retardates and were, in this respect, more like the normal spellers in the sort of spelling errors they made. The implication of this sort of finding is that the reading-and-spelling retardates are impaired in the ability to spell using sound-to-print conversion rules. This conclusion is similar to the one reached in the earlier chapter on specific reading retardation which implicated a deficiency of print-to-sound conversion in these children. The spelling-only retardates, on the other hand, appear to be able to utilise sound-to-print conversion rules but do not always select the appropriate spelling for a particular sound.

Some further evidence to support these conclusions comes from the performances of these two types of poor spellers at spelling nonsense words like *strind, purst,* and *plair.* Although nonsense words such as these sound like plausible English words, they of course are not and so cannot be spelled by consulting a mental lexicon for spelling information. Nonsense words must generally be spelled by sound-to-print conversion rules and so provide a test of a child's ability to spell using the mechanism. However, nonsense words might also be spelled by analogy – a strategy which combines sound-to-print rules and lookup of the mental lexicon. Table 7.2 summarises the results of two studies that have examined the spelling of nonsense words. Given that the spelling-only retardates and the reading-and-spelling retardates are both poor at spelling, there is an interesting difference in their performance with the nonsense words. The performance of the spelling-only retardates falls in between that of the reading-and-spelling retardates and the normal spellers. The particularly poor performance of the reading-and-spelling retardates confirms our earlier conclusion that these children tend to have a problem with sound-to-print conversion.

However, there is another aspect of spelling nonsense words which provides some interesting clues to the nature of the spelling deficit in the spelling-only retardates. Uta Frith (1980) made the interesting observation that good spellers are in remarkable agreement as to

Table 7.2 Percentage of nonsense words spelled correctly by normal and retarded spellers

Study	Normal spellers %	Spelling-only retardates %	Reading-and-spelling retardates %
Frith (1980)	93	85	67
Jorm (1981)	72	53	50

what they consider the correct spelling of nonsense words to be. Retarded spellers, on the other hand, do not agree to the same extent. To understand this point it is important to remember that nonsense words do not have a single correct spelling. Thus, *purst* and *perst, plair* and *plare* are equally correct. However, nonsense words are spelled in certain ways much more commonly than others. Frith referred to these common spellings as *conventional responses* and to the unusual, but still correct, spellings as *unconventional responses*. As an example of these different types of responses Frith gives the following spellings of the nonsense word *usterand:*

Type of response	*Example*
Phonetically accurate – conventional	USTERAND
Phonetically accurate – unconventional	ASTERAND
Phonetically inaccurate	AUSTERAN

Table 7.3 shows the percentage of each type of response in Frith's study. Note that the unconventional, but phonetically accurate responses, are more common amongst the spelling-only retardates. So even in spelling nonsense words there seems to be some mechanism which allows the speller to select one spelling as preferable to another, even when there are several spellings which are correct on purely phonetic grounds. Frith suggests that these conventional spellings are selected on the basis of analogy with real words, e.g., *usterand* is spelled the way it is by analogy with *understand*. However, there is as yet no direct evidence that analogies form the basis of such conventional spellings. There may be other factors involved in pro-

Table 7.3 Types of misspellings shown by normal and retarded spellers

Type of misspelling	Normal spellers %	Spelling-only retardates %	Reading-and-spelling retardates %
Phonetically accurate – conventional	90	75	60
Phonetically accurate – unconventional	3	10	7
Phonetically inaccurate	7	15	33

ducing conventional spellings such as the various orthographic rules we referred to earlier.

It is interesting to consider whether people with a spelling-only retardation would exist with a language which had a simple regular correspondence between sounds and spellings. In an ideal spelling system of this sort, there would be only one possible spelling for each sound and hence no problem of selecting the appropriate spelling from a range of possibilities. Of course, no such spelling system exists in practice, but there certainly are languages where the spelling system follows simpler correspondences than in English. Unfortunately, virtually all research on spelling has been carried out in English-speaking countries, so we have no evidence as to whether spelling-only retardation is less of a problem in other languages.

The reading process of spelling-only retardates

Why is it that spelling-only retardates lack a knowledge of the appropriate spellings where there are several plausible alternatives? One interesting suggestion made by Uta Frith (1980) is that we acquire this sort of orthographic knowledge as we read and that there is something different about the reading of spelling-only retardates which prevents them from learning it efficiently. At first glance, this view seems to be a strange one because spelling-only retardates are, by definition, children who read normally but have difficulties with spelling. How then can their spelling problems be attributed to the way they read? However, Frith argues that normal spellers and spelling-only retardates may achieve the same reading level by using different reading strategies. Specifically, she suggests that normal spellers and spelling-only retardates are equally good at reading for meaning, but the spelling-only retardates are worse at converting written words to sound.

Let us look briefly at some of the evidence which Frith cites to support her view. First, in an earlier study Frith (1978) found that spelling-only retardates were poorer at reading nonsense words than normal spellers. Frith constructed a nonsense word reading test in which each nonsense word was designed to test a single letter-sound rule. For example, *knobbege* was designed to test the rule that in initial *kn-* the *k* is silent. To be marked as correct, the children had only to pronounce the part of the nonsense word which tested the rule – the rest of the nonsense word being ignored. Using this method of scoring, Frith found that the normal spellers knew the rules for 90 per cent of the words, but the spelling-only retardates knew only 73 per cent. This finding indicates a slight difficulty in converting print to sound by the spelling-only retardates.

In the same study, Frith also had the children read through a list of phrases, putting a tick against those that made sense and a cross against those that did not. Here are some examples of the phrases she used:

please wait for me (✓)

don't forget to write (✓)

bigger that a horse (X)

the time war near (X)

Notice that the senseless phrases contain an inappropriate word which looks very similar to a word which would make sense in the context. With this task, which involved reading for meaning, the spelling-only retardates were as fast and accurate as the normal spellers. However, in a similar task which required the children to place a tick next to those phrases which *sounded* as if they made sense a different pattern of results emerged. Some examples of the phrases used in this task are:

By her a present (✓)

She was there mother (✓)

A gloss of wine (X)

The rain his stopped (X)

Obviously, this task requires the child to convert the printed phrases to sound and in this case the spelling-only retardates were found to be slower and made more errors.

Frith (1980) believes that this difficulty in print-to-sound conversion might affect the child's ability to pick up information about spelling. To see how this might be so, recall that words are read by two different mechanisms operating in parallel. Thus, a word might be simultaneously processed both as a visual whole and by a letter-based conversion to sound. However, only the holistic processing is strictly necessary for the word to be correctly identified. In a sense, the detailed letter-based analysis is redundant in that it is unnecessary for word identification, but the habitual use of this mechanism may help a child acquire knowledge of the orthographic patterns of the written language. Frith's argument is that spelling-only retardates lack a full knowledge of orthographic patterns because they do not use the redundant but detailed reading mechanism which would allow them to acquire this knowledge. To use Frith's own terminology, the normal speller reads by 'full cues', while the spelling-only retardate reads by 'partial cues'.

Although use of a 'partial cue' strategy seems to be adequate for reading, it does not work so well for spelling. When reading a familiar word we can process its whole visual form simultaneously. In fact, we can identify a word correctly even with some of the visual information missing, as in RE D NG or R C MM ND. The only time a reader has to attend to all the detailed information in a word is when it is unfamiliar, as in reading nonsense words.

Spelling differs from reading in that letters must be produced one at a time. A spelling cannot be produced by the simultaneous method used in reading. Furthermore, to spell a word correctly, we must produce every letter in its correct order. Omitting letters is not an acceptable strategy. In short, spelling is a sequential process which requires complete knowledge of a word's letter structure. A child who lacks detailed knowledge about a familiar word may easily manage to read it correctly, but will have great difficulty spelling it. If Frith is right, the spelling-only retardate may be such a person.

The cognitive deficit in spelling retardation

We have seen that there are differences in the nature of the spelling deficit between children who have difficulties specifically in spelling and children who have difficulties in both reading and spelling. It might be expected that the two groups would also differ in their pattern of basic cognitive abilities, and there is now a reasonable amount of evidence to show that this is the case.

Nelson and Warrington (1974) compared the intelligence test results of reading-and-spelling and spelling-only retardates using the Wechsler Intelligence Scale for Children. Recall that this test is divided into two broad sections: a scale dealing with language-related abilities which yields a Verbal IQ, and a scale dealing with non-language abilities which yields a Performance IQ. Nelson and Warrington's results are shown in Table 7.4. The first thing to look at in this table is the degree of reading and spelling retardation shown by the two groups. Both groups were, on average, over three years behind other children of their age in spelling. However, with reading the picture is somewhat different: the reading-and-spelling retardates are over three years behind, but the spelling-only retardates are less than a year behind. Next, look at the average Verbal and Performance IQs of the two groups. The spelling-only retardates in this study are a rather bright group, with average IQs of well above 100 on both

Table 7.4 Intellectual abilities of spelling retardates

	Spelling-only retardates	Reading-and-spelling retardates
No. of children in the group	17	54
Average years behind in reading	.67	3.47
Average years behind in spelling	3.16	3.88
Average verbal IQ	114	99
Average performance IQ	118	113
Difference between verbal and performance IQs	–4	–14

the Verbal and Performance Scales. Also, their Verbal IQs and Performance IQs are rather similar, with the Performance IQ being only four points higher on average. However, with the reading-and-spelling retardates, the picture is completely different. They performed well on the Performance scale, but are slightly below the group average on the Verbal Scale. In fact, their Performance IQ is an average of fourteen points above their Verbal IQ. In short, the reading-and-spelling retardates seem to have a general deficit in language abilities which the spelling-only retardates do not have.

Other studies provide confirming evidence that reading-and-spelling retardates have a language ability deficit which the spelling-only retardates do not have. A later study by Sweeney and Rourke (1978) used a somewhat different approach, but arrived at a rather similar conclusion. They selected a group of 9-10 year olds and a group of 13-year-olds who were poor at spelling. They then classified these children into two groups according to whether their spelling errors were predominantly of the phonetically accurate or phonetically inaccurate variety. Although both phonetically accurate and phonetically inaccurate spellers were equally bad at spelling, the phonetically accurate spellers were found to be better at reading, confirming the finding that phonetically accurate spelling errors are associated with a deficit in spelling but not in reading. The two groups of poor spellers were given a large number of tests involving language-related abilities. These tests included the various subtests from the Verbal scale of the Wechsler Intelligence Scale for Children, as well as other tests such as Auditory Discrimination of Speech Sounds, Sentence Memory, and Verbal Fluency.

Over all, the phonetically inaccurate spellers tended to be worse on these language ability tests than the phonetically accurate spellers. However, whereas this difference in language abilities was marked with the older children, it was only slight with the younger ones. A graph of Sweeney and Rourke's findings is shown in Figure 7.1. This result indicates that the presence of phonetically inaccurate errors is indicative of a general language-ability deficit in older children, but not necessarily in younger children.

In conclusion, we have seen that reading-and-spelling retardates have a generalised deficit in language-related abilities. However, the nature of the deficit in spelling-only retardates is still unclear. Although we know that spelling-only retardates do not have the same general deficit in language abilities, nobody has yet discovered

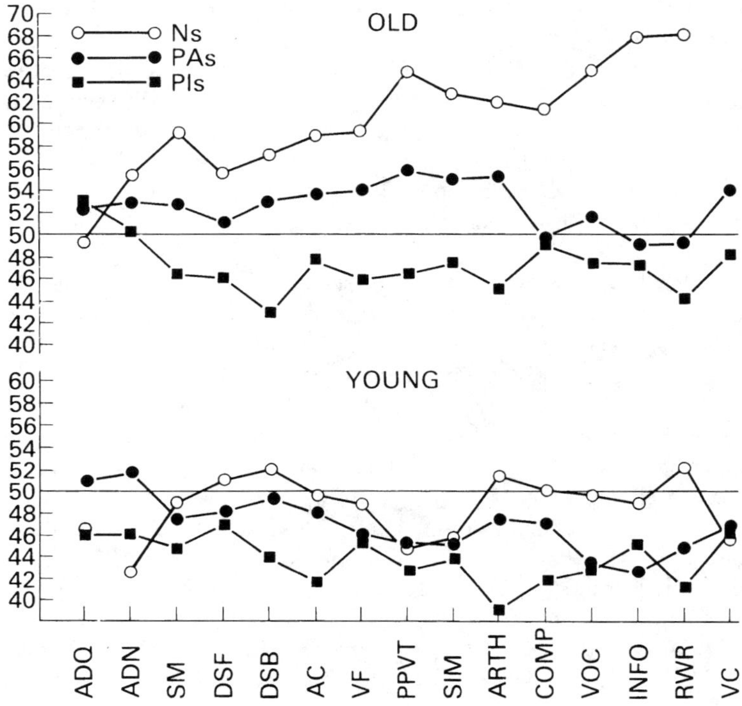

Figure 7.1
Language abilities of normal (N), phonetically accurate (PA) and phonetically inaccurate (PI) spellers
Source: Sweeney and Rourke, 1978.

whether they have some sort of other more subtle cognitive deficit. The understanding of the basis for their spelling disability remains an important task for the future research.

8 Remediation, prediction and prevention

Much is now known about the nature and causes of literacy problems, but unfortunately this knowledge has not had a great deal of impact on our ability to overcome these problems. However, there are some encouraging signs that successful treatment programmes can be developed. In this chapter, we will look at the broad types of programmes that have been proposed, their theoretical rationale, and their success to date.

One very general feature of all the treatment programmes we will examine is that they have been aimed at an undifferentiated group of poor readers. There has been no attempt to differentiate these children according to more specific reading deficits. This situation provides a good example of the failure of basic research to influence the development of treatment programmes. It also partly reflects the fact that we as yet know very little about some types of literacy problems, such as specific comprehension or spelling difficulties.

Approaches to remediation

One broad class of treatment approaches attempts to take children who are behind in reading and give them some sort of extra teaching which will help them to catch up with other children their age. These *remedial programmes* are essentially designed to correct reading problems after they have developed. Although all remedial programmes share the same basic philosophy of intervening after reading problems have developed, there are a number of quite different approaches to how remediation should be carried out. We will distinguish three major approaches, but this should not be taken to imply that all remedial programmes fit neatly into one of these three categories.

Perhaps the most straightforward approach to remediation might be referred to as *direct instruction*. In this approach, it is assumed that the child having reading difficulties has failed to acquire certain basic reading skills because of inadequate instruction and that he or she needs to go back and learn these skills properly. This approach accords well with commonsense – assess what the child does not know and then teach it. In effect, this strategy means that the slower learner receives the same instructional approach as the fast learner but gets to spend more time at mastering certain stages of the reading curriculum which cause particular difficulties. Engelmann (1967) is an advocate of this approach. He offers the following advice to teachers:

> be cautious about assuming that different children 'learn in a different way' and must be treated differently. If the criterion of performance is the same for all children, the steps they must take to arrive at that criterion must be the same; therefore, the instruction should be basically the same, in that it should concentrate on the skills that the children must learn in order to achieve the desired criterion of performance (which is to be able to translate clusters of symbols into words) (p. 200).

As we will see, Engelmann's advice is in sharp contrast to the philosophies of the other two approaches to remediation that are described below.

A second approach to remediation assumes that if a child fails to achieve adequately in reading it is because he or she has some fundamental cognitive disability. According to this approach, it is not enough simply to give the child more reading instruction because the basic cognitive deficits which caused the reading problem in the first place will still be present.

Rather, the basic cognitive disabilities must themselves be remediated by appropriate training so that the block to normal reading acquisition is removed. This approach to remediation will be referred to as *prerequisite skills training.* The following case report from Tansley (1967) illustrates the application of this sort of approach.

> SH Boy CA 9 3/12 years Reading: Nil
> WISC Verbal IQ = 62. Performance IQ = 44.
> Full IQ = 47.
> (High Vocabulary Score.)
> Strong evidence from neurological examination, case history, and perceptual tests of brain damage and neurological abnormality. His main weaknesses in perception are in visual and

auditory rhythm and visual-motor activity. His drawing of a man indicates lack of awareness of body parts and body schema; laterality has not been thoroughly established.

He is already having a programme designed to assist neurological organization and to improve awareness of his own body.

He is also having perceptual training. Every opportunity should be taken to supplement this work in the classroom situation, e.g., by talking to him, getting him to model in plasticine and to explore things haptically.

There are signs of perseveration.

He is hyperactive and efforts should be made to slow him down, e.g., by giving quiet, slow instructions and insisting on slow, clearly enunciated answers and conversation, and slower, more precise movements.

He is not ready for reading, but already improvements are obvious, e.g., he can now match words as a visual discrimination exercise. I am hopeful that this boy will make eventual progress when we have concentrated on his neurology and perception

(January 1967. Now made successful start to reading) (p. 163).

A third broad approach focuses on direct reading instruction rather than prerequisite skills training, yet takes account of the child's basic cognitive deficit. According to this approach, each child's reading instruction should be matched to fit his or her pattern of cognitive abilities. In other words, children with one pattern of cognitive abilities would be taught by a method ideally suited to them, while children with a different pattern of cognitive abilities would be taught by another method. That is, the method of reading instruction is individualised to suit the child. This type of approach could be perhaps summed up by the motto: 'Teach to the child's strengths.' This approach will be referred to as *compensatory teaching*. It is based around a notion which is technically known as *aptitude-treatment interaction*. According to this notion, basic cognitive skills (aptitudes) and method of instruction (treatment) interact with each other to determine a child's level of reading achievement. Of course, when children are initially taught to read at school, the teacher usually gives all children in the class the same method of instruction irrespective of their pattern of basic cognitive abilities. For some children the particular method of instruction chosen may happen to be the ideal method, but for other children it may not be. These latter children will then fail to achieve as well as they might and may become labelled as retarded readers. To remediate their difficulty it will be best to teach them using a method which is better suited to their pattern of cognitive abilities. The following quotation from Naidoo (1970) illustrates how the notion of compensatory teaching is used in devising individually tailored remedial programmes:

> George is the third child in a family of five children. Father is a factory worker and mother works part-time. One of George's elder brothers has considerable reading difficulty. Pregnancy and birth were normal. Mother's blood is Rhesus negative. George was not late in walking or beginning to use language but articulation was always indistinct.
>
> When seen first at the Centre, George had been in a remedial class for two years but was still quite unable to read or spell, his reading age being five years four months and spelling age five years one month. He was a shy lad, not forthcoming in conversation and at first rather nervous. However, good rapport was established with the examiner. George was interested in tasks presented, and concentrated upon them well and for a considerable duration of time. Verbal expression was poor. Not only were minor articulatory deficits still present but George frequently mispronounced words by twisting the order of sounds within them. 'Signal' was given as 'single', 'another' as 'ovens' (articulatory and sequential error). He found it difficult to find the right word in conversation.
>
> The WISC revealed a high average ability for verbal reasoning, an average for age vocabulary but a marked deficit for the immediate recall of an orally presented sequence of digits.
>
> His arithmetic score was also very low. There was no evidence of any visuo-perceptual difficulty. His performance on a test of visual recall was well within normal limits for age and IQ. George's ability to discriminate between very similar sounds was good. On a test of motor ability George's performance was that of a 6 to 7 year old. Pencil control in drawing and writing was very poor. He had severe directional confusion and had not yet learned to identify right and left either in relation to his own body or in extra-personal space. He used the right hand for writing but the left a great deal in other activities. He was right-eyed and right-footed. In spite of the finding that his Verbal

IQ was a few points higher than Performance IQ, George's difficulties lay predominantly in the expressive language areas and in his very poor recall for a sequence of sounds. His strengths lay in perceiving and recalling visually presented material.

This pattern of strength and deficit areas was still clearly evident in the ITPA given almost a year later when George became a pupil at the Centre. The implications of these strengths and deficits for developing a programme to meet George's needs are clear. When tuition began he lacked sufficient skill in word analysis and sound synthesis to benefit from a phonic approach. By the time he could decode the last letter of a three- or four-letter word, he would have forgotten what the first sound was. But he could recognise and recall visual patterns. So his teacher began by using a whole-word approach and quite soon George had acquired a respectable sight vocabulary.

In such children the visual strengths must be fully utilised in building up a sight vocabulary, and an approach which may be described as 'Say and Look' is more helpful than 'Look and Say' to the child who finds it difficult to recall sounds and words. Using a 'Say and Look' approach one begins with two or three words supplied by the pupil, preferably names of objects of interest to him which he can draw. The teacher prints each word on a separate card and the first association between the word pattern and word sound is established using the child's own pictures. Later a direct association between visual pattern and word is created by placing all cards in front of the child. The teacher then says one of the words and asks the pupil to point to the word spoken. The teacher 'Says', thus providing that part of the link which the pupil has difficulty in recalling, and the pupil 'Looks' using his known ability to recognise patterns. Only when the association between pattern and sound appears to be firmly established using this approach does one introduce 'Look and Say' in the conventional way.

Visual strengths are used in dealing with words with similar sounds and visual units. Children like George find great difficulty in understanding what a rhyme is and hear no similarity between the sounds of the word 'small' and 'tall' for example. However, if one writes a list of words (three or four are sufficient) all containing a common sound/symbol unit, such as 'small', 'fall', 'call', they can identify the common visual units. Having discovered for themselves that these words have something in common, children can use this new knowledge to identify the common sound unit (Naidoo, 1970, pp. 46-7).

Evaluating the effectiveness of remediation

Now let us look at some of the problems involved in evaluating the effectiveness of these various approaches to remediation. Although in the discussion that follows it might appear that we are digressing unnecessarily into details of methodology and experimental design, there is good reason for doing so. Parents and teachers sometimes become enthusiastic proponents of a particular remedial programme after reading seemingly impressive evidence for its effectiveness. However, more often than not the evidence purporting to show the effectiveness of the approach is completely inadequate. Unfortunately, these inadequacies are often not obvious to the layman, nor sometimes to the professional. It is therefore worthwhile digressing to look at what sort of evidence is needed to say that a remedial programme is indeed effective.

Many studies evaluating remedial programmes claim that instruction is effective if the children in the programme gain more in reading achievement than would otherwise be expected. For example, if a 12 year old child has a reading age of 9.0 at the start of remedial instruction and after six months in the programme has a reading age of 9.9, it might be claimed that the remediation was successful because the child has gained 9 months in reading age over a period of only 6 months. Although this method of evaluating the effectiveness of remedial programmes is widely used, it is based on the false assumption that a child who is behind in reading would be expected to gain only x months of reading age after x months without any remedial instruction. The reason why this assumption is false is not easy to understand. Basically, it ignores what is known in statistics as the *regression effect*. One of the consequences of the regression effect is that any group of people who are selected because they get extreme scores on a test will tend to appear more like the average (they 'regress' toward the average) if tested a second time. This effect of regressing toward the average has to do with the imperfect nature of the tests used to assess reading achievement. In the case of poor readers, this means that they will tend to show some improvement if retested a second time, irrespective of whether the events that have intervened between the first and second tests have had any effect on their reading abilities. In other words, a child might gain nine months in reading age over a period of six months' remedial instruction and yet, in actual fact, have gained nothing from the remediation. The apparent gain would be just an illusion caused by the inability of our tests to measure reading achievement perfectly.

To evaluate properly the effects of remediation, we need to know what happens to poor readers who receive no remediation. For a remedial programme to be successful it must produce gains in reading achievement over and above those which would occur anyway as a result of other factors such as standard classroom instruction. The usual method of assessing what would happen anyway is to have a *control group* of poor readers who receive no remedial instruction and are used as a baseline against which the effects of a remedial programme can be assessed. In a typical study, a group of poor readers would be selected by some standard procedure. Half of these children would be randomly assigned to the control group and the other half assigned to the treatment group. Both groups would be pre-tested for reading achievement and then the treatment group would begin to receive remediation. After the remedial programme was completed, both groups of children would be given a post-test to assess any change in reading achievement. If the treatment group was found to have gained substantially more than the control group we could conclude that the remedial programme was effective. Although evaluation of remedial programmes often stops at this point, there is really one further step we need to take in order to be sure that remedial instruction is effective. We need to evaluate whether the programme has any long-term effects. It is possible that the children in a treatment group outperform the children in a control group immediately after a remedial programme has finished, but this does not necessarily mean that they will still be ahead in two years time. Once remediation ceases, the children in the control group might gradually catch up. If this were the case, the remedial programme would have to be regarded as ineffective in the long term. In short, we also need to assess the long-term effects of a remedial programme to evaluate its effectiveness properly. Unfortunately, very few evaluation studies take this last important step.

Having seen what constitutes an adequate evaluation of a remedial programme, let us see how successful various approaches to remediation have been found to be. The straightforward direct instruction approach has proved to be the most successful to date. Programmes of this type are sometimes found to have long-term effects on reading achievement. Nevertheless, in many cases children who are given this form of remedial instruction are found to be superior to control children at the end of treatment, but the two groups gradually converge in reading achievement as time goes on (Carroll, 1972). Obviously, there must be something different about those direct instruction programmes which succeed in producing long-term advantages compared to those which produce only short-term advantages. Guthrie, Seifert and Kline (1978) have looked at various programmes of this sort in an attempt to discern the characteristics of those programmes which are most successful. They concluded that the length of a remedial programme was a crucial factor in producing long-term advantages. Programmes which involved 50 hours or more of instruction produced long-term advantages, whereas shorter programmes produced only short-term advantages. There was also some indication that remedial instruction is more likely to have long-term effects if it is distributed over a long period with a few hours of instruction per week rather than massed into a short period of intensive instruction.

Probably the least effective programmes have been those which have concentrated on prerequisite skills training rather than on reading instruction per se. Although remedial programmes of this type might lead to increases in scores on tests of basic cognitive skills, this generally has no carry-over to the child's reading (see Hammill, Goodman and Weiderholt, 1974). One reason for the failure of these programmes may be that they generally concentrate on training visual and motor skills (which are not generally found to be deficient in poor readers), rather than the linguistic skills which research has shown to be important. For example, if phonological memory skills were trained a different result might emerge.

The success of the compensatory teaching approach is as yet uncertain. The general notions behind this approach to remediation are quite sensible, but at this stage nobody has discovered how to tailor reading instruction to fit in with a child's abilities. For most children, initial reading instruction which emphasises letter-sound relationships (phonics methods) is generally found to be superior to that which emphasises reading whole words for meaning (Chall, 1967; Pflaum, Walberg, Karegianes and Rasher, 1980). However, there may be a minority of children for whom the opposite is true. For example, a study by Stallings (1970) supports this contention. She found that children who had a good short-term memory span were best taught to read by a type of phonics method, while children with a poor short-term memory span were best taught by a method emphasising whole words. However, most other research attempting to fit teaching methods to children's abilities has failed to produce any clear-cut results. Part of the reason for the failure of this approach so far may be that people have attempted to relate reading instruction to abilities that have little to do with reading. For example, there have been unsuccessful attempts to individualise reading instruction according to a child's preference for learning through different senses, particularly, vision, touch, and hearing (Derevensky, 1978). However, preferences for learning through sensory modalities may not be a sensible basis for individualising reading instruction. Despite the popularity of this approach, there are really no grounds in either theory or research for expecting that sensory modality preferences should have any relationship to the best method of reading instruction for an individual child. Until advocates of compensatory teaching begin to base instruction around abilities which have some real relevance to the reading process, it is unlikely that this approach will be effective. However, the compensatory teaching approach remains a promising one for the future and should not be peremptorily dismissed because of its failures to date.

Prediction of reading difficulties

Although remedial instruction is of great importance for the child who is having difficulties with reading, it would be far better if such difficulties could be prevented in the first place so that remediation was unnecessary. The basic problem with attempting to prevent reading difficulties from developing in the first place is that we only know a child is having problems when he or she has been undergoing formal reading instruction for some time. However, there is a way around this problem. As we have seen in an earlier chapter, children with reading difficulties are frequently characterised by certain cognitive deficits. If these cognitive deficits are present before the child begins formal reading instruction, then we have a means of predicting whether a child is likely to have difficulties in learning to read. Of course, simply because a child performs poorly on certain cognitive tasks would not guarantee that he or she is going to have reading problems, nor would excellent performance on these cognitive tasks guarantee success in learning to read. There are many factors besides a child's basic cognitive abilities which influence degree of success at reading. These include the amount and quality of instruction at school, types of language stimulation in the home, and the possession of social skills such as being able to sit still and pay attention. Nevertheless, by measuring a child's cognitive abilities at the beginning of formal reading instruction, we might be able to make predictions about future reading problems which are sufficiently accurate to be useful.

Several attempts have been made to develop batteries of cognitive tests which can be administered to the pre-school child for the purposes of predicting later reading difficulties. We will look at one of these attempts in some detail. This particular study, by Jansky and de Hirsch (1972), is among the best of its kind. Jansky and de Hirsch gave a battery of 19 different cognitive ability tests to a group of 500 Kindergarten children in New York City. Most of these children were 5 years old at the time of this testing. The 19 tests administered to the children are listed in Table 8.1. These tests covered the broad range of cognitive skills which Jansky and de Hirsch thought might be relevant to reading acquisition. When the children reached Grade 2, Jansky and de Hirsch were able to locate and test 400 of the original 500. They gave these children a number of reading and spelling tests with the aim of relating their achievement to performance on the battery of tests administered in Kindergarten. Jansky and de Hirsch used the statistical technique of multiple regression to select out the set of Kindergarten tests which in combination gave the best prediction of Grade 2 reading achievement. The following set of 5 tests was found to do the best job at predicting:

1 Letter Naming.
2 Picture Naming.
3 Word Matching.
4 Bender Motor Gestalt.
5 Sentence Memory.

These tests are quite a heterogeneous collection. Some would be measures of early reading knowledge (Letter Naming, Word Matching), others probably reflect phonological memory skills (Picture Naming, Sentence Memory), and another seems to be a measure of spatial ability (Bender Motor Gestalt). Although these 5 tests in combination were the best set of predictor tests out of the total battery of 19 tests, virtually all of the tests had some relationship to later reading achievement. However, it was found that tests of oral

Table 8.1 Tests administered by Jansky and de Hirsch (1972) to kindergarten children

Test name	*Brief description*
1 Pencil Use	Assesses whether the child can use a pencil to write effectively.
2 Name Writing	Tests whether a child can spell his or her first name correctly.
3 Bender Motor Gestalt Test	Requires the child to copy geometric drawings.
4 Minnesota Percepto-Diagnostic Test	Tests the child's ability to copy designs.
5 Tapped Patterns	The child has to copy a pattern of loud and soft taps.
6 Sentence Memory	Requires the child to hold sentences in short-term memory.
7 Wepman Auditory Discrimination Test	Requires the child to say whether pairs of spoken words sound the same or different.
8 Boston Speech Sound Discrimination Test	The child is asked to point to pairs of pictures named by the tester.
9 Roswall-Chall Auditory Blending Test	Requires the child to blend speech sounds into whole words.
10 Oral Language Level	Assesses the maturity of the child's language when telling a story about cartoon sequences.
11 Number of Words Used in Telling a Story	Number of words used in previous test.
12 Category Names	The child is asked to give generic names for groups of words.
13 Picture Names	The child is asked to name pictures of objects.
14 Letter Naming	The child is asked to name some letters.
15 Horst Nonsense Word Matching Test	Tests the child's ability to match sequences of 2 or 3 letters.
16 Word Matching Test	Tests the ability to match written words.
17 Matching by Configuration	Assesses the ease with which the child can match visually identical words.
18 Recognition of Words Previously Taught	The child has to recognise two words taught at the beginning of the testing session.
19 Spelling Two Words Previously Taught	The child has to spell the two words. which were previously taught.

language abilities were generally more highly related to later reading than tests of other abilities – a finding quite consistent with our conclusion in an earlier chapter concerning the importance of phonological memory skills in reading acquisition.

The combination of 5 tests which made the optimal prediction were developed into a final predictive test battery called the Screening Index which could be administered to an individual child in only 15-20 minutes. This Screening Index would give a reasonable indication of whether or not a child might be expected to have later difficuties with reading. Children with low scores on the Screening Index would be expected to do poorly at reading unless given special help. Jansky and de Hirsch found that the Screening Index could correctly identify 77 per cent of the children who were not reading adequately by Grade 2, and it incorrectly picked up only 19 per cent of those children who eventually turned out to be adequate readers.

Unfortunately, Jansky and de Hirsch did not differentiate specific reading retardation from general reading backwardness or any of the specific comprehension and spelling problems distinguished in earlier Chapters. It is possible that different combinations of tests would be relevant to the prediction of each of these problems. Nevertheless, Jansky and de Hirsch's work was a valuable first step and showed that the prediction of reading difficulties can be carried out with enough accuracy to be of use.

Prevention of reading difficulties

Once we can select children who are likely to have problems in learning to read, we are in a position to prevent these problems from arising. There are many possible approaches we might take in a preventative programme. However, these approaches can be grouped into the three broad categories we used when discussing remedial programmes: direct instruction, prerequisite skills training, and compensatory teaching. Preventative programmes of each of these three types have been proposed and there have been a couple of studies evaluating the effectiveness of such programmes. We will now look at examples of these three types of preventative programmes in terms of their content and effectiveness.

The first type of preventative programme involves direct instruction in reading. That is, children who are considered likely to be slower at learning to read are given extra instruction to help them keep up. A programme of this type has been developed and evaluated by Wallach and Wallach (1976). Children in this programme are selected on the basis of low scores on a reading readiness test which assesses knowledge of letters and sentences. These children are given individual tutoring in reading by adults from the local community who are paid for the job. These adults do not need to have any previous experience or training as teachers. They are simply given three weeks of training in the use of Wallach and Wallach's reading programme. This programme places heavy emphasis on phonics. It consists of three levels:

1. Learning to recognise the shapes of letters and the sounds they represent.
2. Learning to sound out simple words.
3. Reading simple stories.

At each of these levels there are a number of teaching activities which the child proceeds through. These activities are arranged so that each one builds on the skills learned in previous activities. The child has to master each of these activities before proceeding on to the next one in the sequence. The basic principles behind this programme are (a) to proceed in small carefully arranged steps and (b) make sure the child masters each step along the way before proceeding to the next one.

Wallach and Wallach evaluated their programme in two inner-city Chicago schools having predominantly black students. All children entering first grade were given a reading readiness test and those with low scores were randomly assigned to either a treatment group or a control group. The children in the treatment group were given extra individual tutoring by some mothers from the local community, while the children in the control group received only the standard classroom reading instruction. Altogether the children in the treatment group received tutoring for half an hour per school day over about thirty weeks. At the end of the school year, the two groups were compared on a number of reading tests and it was found that the treatment group had made significantly greater progress in reading. Unfortunately, there was no assessment of whether or not these gains were maintained after the treatment programme was terminated. Unless the treatment group continued to be ahead throughout the rest of their schooling, the preventative programme could not be deemed successful. More recently, the Wallach programme has been implemented and evaluated in a school in a different region of the United States by Dorval, Wallach and Wallach (1978). The programme was found to be just as effective as in the original evaluation, but again no long-term follow-up was carried out. At this stage, the results of the Wallach programme look very promising, but we must withhold our final judgment on its worth until long-term maintenance of effects has been demonstrated.

A preventative programme which emphasises the training of prerequisite skills has been developed by Hagin, Silver and Kreeger (1976) in New York. They have named their programme TEACH. The TEACH programme is meant to be used in conjunction with a battery of predictive tests known as the SEARCH battery (Silver and Hagin, 1976). SEARCH consists of ten different tests which are supposed to measure various aspects of perception. It is meant to be given individually to children at the beginning of first grade and takes about 20 minutes to administer and score. If a child gets low scores on 5 or more of the 10 tests then it is considered likely that he or she will have difficulties in learning to read. In order to prevent these difficulties developing, the child is given special 'perceptual stimulation' in the areas of deficit revealed by the SEARCH battery. This perceptual stimulation is achieved using the special learning tasks of the TEACH programme. These learning tasks are organised into the five clusters shown in Table 8.2. Once the child's basic areas of perceptual deficiency are strengthened, he or she is supposed to be able to handle reading with less difficulty.

The basic orientation towards prerequisite skills training is illustrated by Hagin, Silver and Kreeger's description of the case of Norma:

> The profile for Norma illustrates a high-visual/low-auditory pattern. This is a child who experiences difficulty in discriminating sounds and in ordering elements within a sequence. These skills have direct implications for word attack skills in reading. They may also influence the development of accurate articulation, as in Norma's profile. Because of the importance of auditory skills to these two aspects of the language arts, these areas should have high priority on the teaching plan (p. 6).

A thorough evaluation of the TEACH programme has been carried out in the United States by Arnold, Barnebey, McManus, Smeltzer, Conrad, Winer, and Desgranges (1977). These researchers gave the SEARCH battery to all the first-grade children in three schools. This testing located 86 children who had low SEARCH scores and were considered vulnerable to having difficulties in learning to read.

Table 8.2 Clusters of tasks used in the TEACH programme

Task cluster	*Description of tasks*
Visual cluster	Teaches visual discrimination and recall, visual sequencing and visual figure-background.
Visual-motor cluster	Teaches the basic motor patterns that underlie writing.
Auditory cluster	Teaches progressively finer discriminations and recall of sounds within words, recognition of rhyming words, and ordering and blending of sounds within words.
Body-image cluster	Teaches total body image concepts, the mapping of finger schema, and the identification of left and right directionality.
Intermodel cluster	Teaches matching of the temporal and spatial position of initial consonant sounds, consonant blends, digraphs, and the association of visual symbols with their auditory equivalents.

A group of 23 of these children were given the TEACH programme. They were tutored individually for two 30 minute sessions each week over a whole school year. Another group of 23 children received regular academic tutoring for the same amount of time each week. These children were individually tutored in reading and mathematics using standard series of textbooks. The other 40 children with low SEARCH scores were not given any special treatment. At the end of first grade, all these groups of children were reevaluated to see how much progress they had made in academic achievement (reading, spelling, arithmetic), perceptual skills (as measured by the SEARCH battery), and social behaviour. They found that the children receiving the TEACH programme tended to show more improvement in all these areas compared to the children receiving regular academic tutoring and the no-tutoring group. However, as has been pointed out previously, the most important criterion for evaluating the success of a remedial or preventative programme is whether its effects persist after the programme has terminated. To assess whether long-term effects had occurred, Arnold and his colleagues retested as many children as they could locate a year after the preventative programme had finished. They were able to retest 74 of the original 86 children who were considered vulnerable to reading difficulties. They found that the group of children who had received the TEACH programme were now even further ahead of the other groups. They had shown significantly more improvement than the regular-academic-tutoring and no-tutoring groups in reading and spelling, but not in arithmetic. Furthermore, they had gained in IQ whereas the other groups had declined somewhat. There were also gains in social behaviour and in SEARCH scores. Overall, the long-term results of the TEACH programme were very impressive. Arnold and his colleagues report that they originally decided to evaluate the TEACH programme because they were skeptical about the results claimed by Silver and Hagin. However, the strong gains they found convinced them of the worthwhileness of this approach to prevention.

Why was the preventative TEACH programme found to be successful whereas remedial programmes based around the notion of prerequisite skills training have been so unsuccessful? The answer may lie in the nature of the prerequisite skills which are trained. Remedial programmes based around prerequisite skills training have often concentrated on visual and motor abilities, when it is language abilities which appear to be deficient in poor readers. However, this does not mean that any programme which concentrates on language abilities will necessarily be successful. Programmes which concentrate on those language skills which are specifically relevant to beginning reading may have more effect on learning to read. In fact, the TEACH programme contains many teaching activities which are directly related to the requirements of learning to read by phonic methods. For example, in one teaching activity, the Show-Me Game, the child is shown a collection of four toys and has to select the appropriate one when the tutor says the sounds of its name. Thus, the tutor might say 'Show me the f-i-s-h' and the child would have to point to the toy fish. This task teaches the child to blend together the component sounds of words, which is a necessary skill for being able to read by letter-sound rules. In other TEACH tasks, the child is taught to match up words which have the same initial or final sounds, to generate rhymes, to associate sounds with letters, to remember letter sequences, and to write letters correctly. Although some of the activities in the TEACH programme appear to train skills which are not directly related to beginning reading, less than half of the activities are of this sort. In other words, the TEACH programme may have been successful because it concentrated largely on training pre-reading skills rather than on basic perceptual abilities. In some respects it is similar in content to Wallach and Wallach's direct instruction programme even though the two programmes are based on rather different philosophies of prevention.

The third broad type of preventative programme involves compensatory teaching – that is, the matching of instructional methods to fit the child's pattern of strengths. Jansky and de Hirsch's (1972) proposals for prevention seem to be basically of this type. Earlier we looked at their Screening Index for predicting future reading difficulties. In addition to the Screening Index, Jansky and de Hirsch developed a Diagnostic Battery which can be used to assess a child's pattern of strengths and weaknesses on basic cognitive tasks relevant to reading acquisition. Children achieving low scores on the Screening Index are then given the Diagnostic Battery to get a detailed picture of their strengths and weaknesses. This result can then be used as a basis for designing suitable preventative teaching programmes.

Jansky and de Hirsch developed the Diagnostic Battery from the 19 cognitive tests used in their predictive study. They employed the statistical technique of factor analysis to group these tests into a smaller number of independent factors. Four factors were found and these were called Visuo Motor Organization, Oral Language, Pattern Matching, and Pattern Memory. The original tests were grouped into these four factors as follows:

Visuo motor organization	*Oral language*	*Pattern matching*	*Pattern memory*
Pencil Use	Picture Naming	Gates Matching	Blending
Bender Gestalt	Oral Language	Nonsense Word Matching	Word Recognition
Name Writing	Categories	Tapped Patterns	Spelling
Spelling	Sentence Memory	Sentence Memory	Boston Auditory Discrimination
	Boston Auditory Discrimination		Letter Naming
	Letter Naming		

The aim of the Diagnostic Battery is to assess children on each of the 4 factors, rather than on the component tests themselves. To achieve this end, children are assigned ratings of *high, medium,* or *low* on each test. A child who receives consistently *high* ratings on the tests which make up a particular factor is regarded as having a strength in that factor, while a child who receives consistently *low* ratings is regarded as having a weakness.

The way in which the Diagnostic Battery can be used to guide the formulation of a preventative teaching programme is illustrated by Jansky and de Hirsch's description of the case of Sally:

> Sally's reputation preceded her. Her pleasant and very young kindergarten teacher told us that in the course of the entire kindergarten year Sally had never been heard to speak to any adult. We learned that very occasionally she would whisper to other children. The teacher frankly thought it would be a waste of time to test her. However, Sally, a pretty black girl, was quite ready to come and smiled in a friendly way. At first she remained mute, though she nodded in answer to questions. We suggested that she whisper to us, as she did to her classmates, and Sally was willing to try.
>
> Testing showed that her reluctance to talk was related to her severe oral-language deficit. Her memory for sentences was poor, her ability to discriminate between similar-sounding words was inferior, her word-finding difficulties were massive, and the stories she told were fragmented and short. However, she managed the pencil well, copied designs nicely, and was moderately proficient at matching and spelling words previously taught. Sally's strengths clearly fell in the Visuo Motor and verbal Pattern Memory areas. There was no doubt as to her marked weakness in Oral Language and in verbal Pattern Matching, both crucial for reading ....
>
> In Sally's case an early educational approach might have used her graphomotor strength and her good pattern memory for learning. She might have been taught to spell certain words; drawing pictures of what they represent would have facilitated recall. At best it would have been difficult for her to move on to contextual reading. The teacher might have written short sentences referring to Sally's own experiences. She would have copied these, memorized them, and then learned the words as sight words in different contexts. To help her remember the words she would have been encouraged to recall how the original *sentence* looked and sounded. Because Sally showed absolutely no aptitude for an analytic approach, initial learning by way of phonics was contraindicated. A modified phonics approach, one based on larger phonemic segments, such as sound families, might well have been attempted later on – only, however, after the child had made a real start in context reading (pp. 86-8).

As yet, only preliminary work has been carried out on the effectiveness of Jansky and de Hirsch's approach (Jansky 1981). This research indicates that the approach shows promise. It was pointed out earlier in this chapter that attempts to match instructional methods to a child's pattern of basic abilities have so far not been very successful. One reason for this failure is that researchers have in most cases attempted to base instruction around basic abilities which are unrelated to the reading process. Jansky and de Hirsch's approach seems to avoid this pitfall, because they have shown that the factors of the Diagnostic Battery do relate to later reading performance. However, until further evaluation is carried out, this approach to prevention must be regarded as the least preferred of the three we have discussed.

The future of prevention

Even from the limited evidence presently on hand, it seems clear that a child's potential for problems in learning to read can be assessed with reasonable accuracy and that this information can be successfully used to prevent these problems from developing. However, there are still many gaps in our knowledge which need to be filled. For example, we do not know whether all types of literacy problems respond equally to prevention. The studies reported to date have not differentiated various types of literacy problems. We need to develop predictive batteries which can indicate the more specific areas of reading and spelling in which a child is likely to develop difficulties, and preventative programmes which meet these specific needs.

The programmes which appear to be successful so far have placed heavy emphasis on instruction in basic skills related to phonics. Although this type of training may be appropriate for a large number of children who are prone to having difficulties in learning to read, it may not be optimal for all. Hopefully, the design of future preventative programmes will be based upon the knowledge gained from fundamental research into the nature of the cognitive deficits involved in such difficulties. There is every reason to be optimistic about the future of prevention. It is not unreasonable to envisage a future in which preventative programmes are so well developed that literacy problems of all types will occur far less frequently than they do today.

References

Arnold, L.E., Barnebey, N., McManus, J., Smeltzer, D.J., Conrad, P., Winer, G., and Desgranges, L. (1977), 'Prevention by specific perceptual remediation for vulnerable first-graders', *Archives of General Psychiatry*, 34, 1279–94.

Baddeley, A.D. and Hitch, G. (1974), Working memory, in G.H. Bower (ed.) *The Psychology of learning and motivation* (vol. 8), New York: Academic Press.

Baker, L. (1979), 'Comprehension monitoring: Identifying and coping with text confusions', *Journal of Reading Behavior*, 11, 365–74.

Biemiller, A. and Bowden, J. (1977), *Predicting reading achievement from picture identification times*. Paper presented at the Convention of the Ontario Educational Research Council, Toronto.

Bransford, J.D. and Johnson, M.K. (1973) Considerations of some problems of comprehension, in W.G. Chase (ed.), *Visual information processing*, New York: Academic Press.

Brown, A.L. and Day, J.D. (1980), *The development of rules for summarizing texts*, unpublished manuscript, University of Illinois, 1980.

Calfee, R.C., Arnold, R. and Drum, P. (1976), Review of *The Psychology of Reading* by Eleanor J. Gibson and Harry Levin, *Proceedings of the National Academy of Education*, 3, 1–80.

Carroll, H.C.M. (1972), 'The remedial teaching of reading: An evaluation', *Remedial Education*, 7, 10–15.

Chall, J. (1967), *Learning to read: The great debate*, New York: McGraw-Hill.

Coles, G.S. (1980), 'Evaluation of genetic explanations of reading and learning problems', *Journal of Special Education*, 14, 365–84.

Coltheart, M., Patterson, K. and Marshall, J.C. (1980), (eds), *Deep dyslexia*, London: Routledge and Kegan Paul.

Conners, C.K. (1970), 'Cortical visual evoked response in children with learning disorders', *Psychophysiology*, 7, 418–28.

Cromer, W. (1970), 'The difference model: A new explanation for some reading difficulties', *Journal of Educational Psychology*, 61, 471–83.

Day, J.D. (1980), *Training summarization skills: A comparison of teaching methods*, unpublished doctoral dissertation, University of Illinois.

Derevensky, J.L. (1978), 'Modal preferences and strengths: Implications for reading research', *Journal of Reading Behavior*, 10, 7–23.

Dorval, B., Wallach, L. and Wallach, M.A. (1978), 'Field evaluation of a tutorial reading program emphasizing phoneme identification skills', *The Reading Teacher,* 31, 784–90.

Einon, Geoff S. (ed.), 'An EEG record', Introduction to the Nervous System, Open University Press, 1974.

Engelmann, S. (1967), 'Teaching reading to children with low mental ages', *Education and Training of the Mentally Retarded,* 2, 193–201.

Finucci, J.M., Guthrie, J.T., Childs, A.L., Abbey, H. and Childs, B. (1976), 'The genetics of specific reading disability', *Annals of Human Genetics,* 40, 1–23.

Firth, I. (1972), *Components of reading disability,* unpublished doctoral dissertation, University of New South Wales.

Frith, U. (1978), 'From print to meaning and from print to sound or how to read without knowing how to spell', *Visible Language,* 12, 43–54.

Frith, U. (1980), Unexpected spelling problems, in U. Frith (ed.)*Cognitive processes in spelling,* London: Academic Press.

Garner, R. (1980), 'Monitoring of understanding: An investigation of good and poor readers' awareness of induced miscomprehension of text', *Journal of Reading Behavior,* 12, 55–63.

Goodman, K. (1967), 'Reading: A psycholinguistic guessing game', *Journal of the Reading Specialist,* 6, 126–36.

Guthrie, J.T. (1973), 'Reading comprehension and syntactic responses in good and poor readers', *Journal of Educational Psychology,* 65, 294–9.

Guthrie, J.T., Seifert, M. and Kline, L.W. (1978), Clues from research on programs for poor readers, in S.J. Samuels (ed.) *What research has to say about reading instruction,* Newark, Delaware: International Reading Association.

Hagin, R.A., Silver, A.A. and Kreeger, H. (1976), *Teach,* New York: Walker Educational Book Corporation.

Hammill, D., Goodman, L. and Weiderholt, J.L. (1974), 'Visual-motor processes: Can we train them?', *The Reading Teacher,* 27, 469–78.

Hanley, J. & Sklar, B. (1976), Electroencephalic correlates of developmental reading dyslexics: Computer analysis of recordings from normal and dyslexic children, in G. Leisman (ed.) *Basic visual processes and learning disability,* Springfield, Illinois: Charles C. Thomas.

Hanna, P.R., Hanna, J.S., Hodges, R.E. and Rudorf, E.H. (1966), *Phoneme-grapheme correspondences as cues to spelling improvement,* Washington, DC.: US Government Printing Office.

Herjanic, B.M. and Penick, E.C. (1972), 'Adult outcome of disabled child readers', *Journal of Special Education,* 6, 397–410.

Hermann, K. (1959), *Reading Disability,* Copenhagen: Munksgaard.

Hewison, J. and Tizard, J. (1980), 'Parental involvement and reading attainment', *British Journal of Educational Psychology,* 50, 209–15.

Hier, D.B., Le May, M., Rosenberger, P.B. and Perlo, V.P. (1978), 'Developmental dyslexia: Evidence for a subgroup with a reversal of cerebral asymmetry', *Archives of Neurology,* 35, 90–2.

Husen, T. (1960), 'Abilities of twins', *Scandinavian Journal of Psychology,* 1, 125–35.

Isakson, R.L. and Miller, J.W. (1976), 'Sensitivity to syntactic and semantic cues in good and poor comprehenders', *Journal of Educational Psychology,* 68, 787–92.

Jansky, J. (1981), 'The clinician in the classroom: a first-grade intervention study', *Bulletin of the Orton Society,* 31, 145–64.

Jansky, J. and de Hirsch, K. (1972), *Preventing reading failure,* New York: Harper & Row.

Jorm, A.F. (1977a), 'Parietal lobe function in developmental dyslexia', *Neuropsychologia,* 15, 841–4.

Jorm, A.F. (1977b), 'Effect of word imagery on reading performance as a function of reader ability', *Journal of Educational Psychology,* 69, 51.

Jorm, A.F. (1981) 'Children with reading and spelling retardation: Functioning of the whole-word and correspondence-rule mechanisms', *Journal of Child Psychology and Psychiatry,* 22, 171–8.

Kintsch, W. and Greene, E. (1978), 'The role of culture-specific schemata in the comprehension and recall of stories', *Discourse Processes,* 1, 1–13.

Kintsch, W. and van Dijk, T.A. (1978), 'Toward a model of discourse comprehension and production', *Psychological Review,* 85, 363–94.

Levin, J.R. (1973), 'Inducing comprehension in poor readers: A test of a recent model', *Journal of Educational Psychology,* 65, 19–24.

McMichael, P. (1979) 'The hen or the egg? Which comes first – Antisocial emotional disorders or reading disability', *British Journal of Educational Psychology,* 49, 226–38.

Makita, K. (1968), 'The rarity of reading disability in Japanese children', *American Journal of Orthopsychiatry,* 38, 599–614.

Mann, V.A., Liberman, I.Y. and Shankweiler, D. (1980), 'Children's memory for sentences and word strings in relation to reading ability', *Memory and Cognition,* 8, 329–35.

Markman, E.M. (1977), 'Realizing that you don't understand: A preliminary investigation', *Child Development,* 48, 986–992.

Marshall, J.C. and Newcombe, F. (1973), 'Patterns of paralexia: A psycholinguistic approach', *Journal of Psycholinguistic Research,* 2, 175–99.

Mason, M., Katz, L. and Wicklund, D.A. (1975), 'Immediate spatial order memory in sixth-grade children as a function of reader ability', *Journal of Educational Psychology,* 67, 610–16.

Matheny, A.P. and Dolan, A.B. (1974), 'A twin study of genetic influences in reading achievement', *Journal of Learning Disabilities,* 7, 99–102.

Naidoo, S. (1970), Remedial re-education, in A.W. Franklin and S. Naidoo (eds), *Assessment and teaching of dyslexic children,* London: Invalid Children's Aid Association.

Nelson, H.E. and Warrington, E.K. (1974), 'Developmental spelling retardation and its relation to other cognitive abilities', *British Journal of Psychology,* 65, 265–74.

Newman, H.H., Freeman, F.N. and Holzinger, K.J. (1937), *Twins: A study of heredity and environment,* University of Chicago Press.

Perfetti, C.A., Goldman, S.R. and Hogaboam, T.W. (1979), 'Reading skill and the identification of words in discourse context', *Memory &*

Cognition, 7, 273–82.

Pflaum, S.W., Walberg, H.J., Karegianes, M.L. and Rasher, S.P. (1980), 'Reading instruction: A quantitative analysis', *Educational Researcher*, 12–18.

Pichert, J.W. and Anderson, R.C. (1977), 'Taking different perspectives on a story', *Journal of Educational Psychology*, 69, 309–15.

Preston, M., Guthrie, J.T. and Childs, B. (1974), 'Visual evoked response in normal and disabled readers', *Psychophysiology*, 11, 452–7.

Preston, M.S., Guthrie, J.T., Kirsch, I., Gertman, D. and Childs, B. (1977), 'VERs in normal and disabled adult readers', *Psychophysiology*, 14, 8–14.

Rozin, P., Poritsky, S. and Sotsky, R. (1971), 'American children with reading problems can easily learn to read English represented by Chinese characters', *Science*, 171, 1264–7.

Rutter, M., Maugham, B., Mortimore, P. and Ouston, J. (1979), *Fifteen thousand hours*, Cambridge, Massachusetts: Harvard University Press.

Rutter, M., Tizard, J. and Whitmore, K. (1970), *Education health and behaviour*, New York: Wiley.

Rutter, M. and Yule, W. (1975), 'The concept of specific reading retardation', *Journal of Child Psychology and Psychiatry*, 16, 181–97.

Rutter, M., Yule, B., Quinton, D., Rowlands, O., Yule, W. and Berger, M. (1975), 'Attainment and adjustment in two geographical areas: III – Some factors accounting for area differences', *British Journal of Psychiatry*, 126, 520–33.

Seymour, P.H.K. and Porpodas, C.D. (1980), Lexical and non-lexical processing of spelling in dyslexia, in U. Frith (ed.) *Cognitive processes in spelling*, London: Academic Press.

Shankweiler, D., Liberman, I.Y., Mark, L.S., Fowler, C.A. and Fischer, F.W. (1979), 'The speech code and learning to read', *Journal of Experimental Psychology: Human Learning and Memory*, 5, 531–45.

Silver, A.A. and Hagin, R.A. (1976), *Search*, New York: Walker Educational Book Corporation.

Smith, F. (1978), *Understanding reading*, 2nd edn, New York: Holt, Rinehart & Winston.

Snowling, M. (1980), 'The development of grapheme-phoneme correspondence in normal and dyslexic readers', *Journal of Experimental Child Psychology*, 29, 294–305.

Spring, C. and Capps, C. (1974), 'Encoding speed, rehearsal, and probed recall of dyslexic boys', *Journal of Educational Psychology*, 66, 780–6.

Stallings, J.A. (1970), *Reading methods and sequencing abilities: An interaction study in beginning reading*, unpublished doctoral dissertation, Stanford University.

Stanovich, K.E. (1980), 'Toward an interactive-compensatory model of individual differences in the development of reading fluency', *Reading Research Quarterly*, 16, 32–71.

Stein, N.L. and Nezworski, T. (1978), 'The effects of organizational and instructional set on story memory', *Discourse Processes*, 1, 177–93.

Sweeney, J.E. and Rourke, B.P. (1978), 'Neuropsychological significance of phonetically accurate and phonetically inaccurate spelling errors in

younger and older retarded spellers', *Brain and Language*, 6, 212–25.
Symann-Lovett, N., Gascon, G.G., Matsumiya, Y. and Lombroso, C.T. (1977), 'Wave form difference in visual evoked responses between normal and reading disabled children', *Neurology*, 27, 156–9.
Tansley, A.E. (1967), *Reading and remedial reading*, London: Routledge & Kegan Paul.
Torgesen, J.K. and Houck, D.J. (1980), 'Processing deficiencies of learning-disabled children who perform poorly on the digit span test', *Journal of Educational Psychology*, 72, 141–60.
Vellutino, F.R., Pruzek, R., Steger, J.A. and Meshoulam, U. (1973), 'Immediate visual recall in poor and normal readers as a function of orthographic-linguistic familiarity', *Cortex*, 9, 368–84.
Vellutino, F.R., Steger, J.A., Harding, C.J. and Phillips, F. (1975), 'Verbal vs. non-verbal paired-associates learning in poor and normal readers', *Neuropsychologia*, 13, 75–82.
Wallach, M.A. and Wallach, L. (1976), *Teaching all children to read*, University of Chicago Press.
Waller, T.G. (1976), 'Children's recognition memory for written sentences: A comparison of good and poor readers', *Child Development*, 47, 90–5.
Warrington, E.K. (1967), 'The incidence of verbal disability associated with reading retardation', *Neuropsychologia*, 5, 175–9.
White, Franklin, A. and Naidoo, S. (eds.), *Assessment and Teaching of Dyslexic Children*, The Invalid Children's Aid Association.
Yule, W. (1973), 'Differential prognosis of reading backwardness and specific reading retardation', *British Journal of Educational Psychology*, 43, 244–8.

Index

Index